RONALD

JESUS IN CORNWALL

The
Secret
Knowledge

BLACKTHORN PUBLISHING

ACKNOWLEDGEMENTS

The Author owes a debt of gratitude to his wife Sylvia Rayner,
Lady of Annesley Grange, Nottinghamshire, for all the
research and translation that made this book possible.

Thanks to Craig Allen Rayner for his creative photography
that make my books attractive.

Front and Back Cover
created by
Craig Allen Rayner

Spiritual Poetry
by
Sylvia Rayner

Creative Photography
by
Craig Allen Rayner

Thanks to L. B. Thornycroft. D. LIT
Thanks to artist Eustace Nash

Rev. R. W. Morgan
Drawings by Horace J. Knowles

Contributions From:
The Voyages of Joseph of Avalon
Joseph Escapes to Glastonbury
The Clintons and the Glastonbury Connection

DISTRIBUTOR
Add Design
Britannia House
Bentwaters Business Park
Rendlesham
Suffolk IP12 2TW
United Kingdom
Telephone: (UK) 01394 460600
E-Mail: info@add-design.co.uk

ISBN 978-0-9557906-3-8

PUBLISHER
Blackthorn Publishing Ltd
Suite 404, Albany House
324-326, Regent Street,
London W1B 3HH
United Kingdom

Printers:
Colt Press Ltd, Unit 7C Perry Road, Witham, Essex CM8 3UD UK

INDEX

INTRODUCTION

THE JESUS SCROLL

Crusader Knights William de Warren, and Rayner the Flemming, unearthed the 'Jesus Scroll' during the construction of what are widely known as the "Crusader Steps" leading down to what is said to be the tomb of Holy Mary in Jerusalem, where her remains were put to rest after being removed from the Kedron Valley. Queen Helena, Roman Empress, and Mother of Constantine the Great ordered the transfer. The tomb is beautiful, and the loving care lavished on the tomb, the floor around the tomb, and the steps leading down to the tomb, is obvious, even in the present day.
Holy Mary's Mother and Father, Ann and Joachim are said to be buried on either side of the steps.

The only place in the known world where mixed Asian and Middle Eastern language scrolls could be translated into a form understood by the Norman French, were the Monasteries of Kyiv, Ukraine.

The early history of that interesting city reveals that Viking raiders travelled down the rivers from Europe towards the Black Sea looking for a place to settle far away from the constant warring in their own lands. These Viking travellers were the true early founders and settlers of the cities of Kyiv and Novgorod. Rurik, a Norseman, became ruler of Kyiv in 850AD.

Not surprisingly, Crusaders with their Viking/Norman ancestry were always happy to travel to Ukraine where they would enjoy a warm reception from a people ruled over by a Christian Prince who supported the Crusader cause. Many in the local population were also aware of their own Viking roots.

In 988AD Vladimir, Prince of Kyiv, had been baptised into Christianity. The Roman Emperor of Constantinople acted as his guide and Godfather. Vladimir set up a Monastery for Christian learning in the woods in Kyiv.
The Crusaders exchanged the original scroll in payment for the translation, plus their shelter and accommodation at the monastery. The Knights set off on their return journey to England with their valuable scroll and to claim their reward from King Stephen. King Stephen gave the scroll to his trusted religious scholar Roger Clinton on his appointment by the King, to the

important position of Bishop of Coventry in 1129. This important event is recorded in an ancient manuscript in the possession of the Author. The manuscript was shown on the famous BBC Antiques Road Show programme and was described by their book expert, Clive Farahar, as priceless.

The translation of the Jesus Scroll reveals that the boy Jesus left Nazareth at the age of twelve years to accompany his wealthy uncle; much respected by the Romans, the Jewish trader and Rabbi Joseph of Arimathea, together with Joseph's youngest son who was around the same age as Jesus and called Adnam Josephus.

The Scroll records that the Prophet Jesus was the Son of Joseph, a carpenter and smithy whose home and extended family were in Galilee. However, Joseph maintained a workshop in Nazareth because of its position on the very busy trade and caravan route to Sepphoris and beyond, a strategy that brought much business into Joseph's workshop. Jesus's three brothers and two sisters, all lived on a farm with their grandparents in Galilee. The grandparents headed an extended family of farmers spread throughout Galilee. All of the members of the family were devoutly religious, and were the driving force in setting up Meeting Houses in the villages throughout Galilee.

John the Baptist, the cousin of Jesus, headed the whole movement. Jesus, being the eldest son, stayed with Joseph and Mary in Nazareth both to help his father in the workshop whilst at the same time learning the trades for which the family were well known.

It was a happy time for Jesus, Joseph and Mary in Nazareth as they went about their daily business, but it was a happy way that was not to last. Troublesome Jewish zealots brought tragedy to the area almost overnight. Sepphoris, a town on a hill about 30 furlongs distant from Nazareth was set ablaze by the Roman Emperor, Herod Antipas, as a punishment for an abortive insurrection and attempt on his life by Jewish zealots.

Two thousand local inhabitants were rounded up and crucified as an example and warning to others. Nazareth, about a one hour walk, was a small place, and there was no way to avoid seeing the corpses rotting on the crosses in the distance at every point on the compass by everyone going about their daily business.

Roman soldiers relentlessly pursued anyone opposed to Roman rule. Everyone faintly under suspicion was arrested, and executed without trial by crucifixion. Joseph and Mary were particularly afraid for their son Jesus, because he was not one to cower before the Roman oppressors. Joseph and Mary decided to take Jesus to the safety of Galilee, to the care of his wealthy uncle, Joseph of Arimathea who was influential in senior Roman circles. A member of the Sanhedrin, and a trader of all sought after commodities, particularly metals. They begged Joseph to take Jesus from Palestine on his next trip to Europe, and keep Jesus abroad with him until such a time that it was safe for Jesus to return to Galilee and Jerusalem.

In the course of his business Joseph travelled extensively to European Ports to barter silk, salt, spices and luxury goods from the Middle East. He would then sail on along the centuries old route to the West Coast of England to satisfy the Romans insatiable desire for metals.

The West coast of England was the golden gateway to the major World source at that time of ferrous and non-ferrous metal ores and metal ingots. These were all essential to the manufacture of Roman armour and weaponry. Bronze was smelted from mixing copper and tin.

Joseph of Arimathea took Jesus, and his own son Adnam Josephus, to the Druid Cor at Glastonbury to benefit from the best education in the world at that time. Joseph returned to Glastonbury in AD38 to build the first Christian Church outside Jerusalem.

DRUIDISM

Druidism remained very active in Britain, Gaul, and Ireland, even in the face of intense persecution by the Romans. Druid High Priests were Counsellors to Kings in all those countries, controlling all sacred functions and matters of religion.

Druidism was a pure religion, because its spirituality was based on worshipping one God, and the belief that the soul of man was immortal, and lived on after death in another; reincarnated to the place and position earned by the manner in which a life had been lived before death. Druids taught the necessity of practicing justice and truth, doing harm to no man, cherishing and protecting little children and being manly at all times. Druids held a vast knowledge of natural medicines. They taught divining as a method of foretelling the future, frequently using the techniques of scrying. Druids studied the stars as a reliable method to ascertaining the seasons for sowing and reaping.

High Priests practiced casting out devils into animals. They successfully used a herb in the palms of the hands to anoint and heal problems of the eyes. Druids also calmed the winds for herring fishermen with a knotted cord. Druids held regular assemblies where they would rule on disputes and legal matters. Druid Priests required students and followers to be present at Druid Services held in groves in forests where the Priests offered burnt sacrifices at an altar, much in the manner of the Jews.

4

DRUID SCHOOLS AT GLASTONBURY

Britain's orthodox Druid Priests and Arch Druids were the natural forerunners in Britain to the Jerusalem Christians and Disciples of Jesus who arrived at the Isle of Avalon in Britain from AD 38. Druids were easily absorbed into Christian Churches when Rome ordered the extermination of Britain's Druids. This is not the story told by Julius Caesar in his writings. My reading of history casts Julius Caesar in the roles of Master of Genocide and Invader and Plunderer of the resources of Europe, slaver of countless numbers of the women and children of the men murdered by his troops. An idol worshipper, a man in my opinion, on a par with Adolf Hitler.

Caesar's writings about the Druids were largely exaggerations, falsifications, and downright lies. All in an effort to cover up and justify the wide spread Roman practice of genocide. In this case the genocide was being perpetrated upon Britain's Druidic tribes. Plus the vile Roman practice of selling off into slavery the wives and children of the Druids murdered by the Roman soldiers. Only after they had been raped, beaten and abused.

Much of the idolatrous filth in Rome around Julius Caesar supported his policy of wiping out Druids, because they saw the Druid Maggi as a capable leadership, with its own religion, independent and defiant towards the rule of Rome. The selling of the Druid wives and orphans was also very profitable for Rome.

Such was the reputation of Druid learning and integrity, that Kings, rulers, and wealthy families around the known world sent their eldest children to study at Druidic schools. The greatest of these seats of learning in Britain was based at Glastonbury located in the West. The system of study in place in Druid schools lasted for up to fifteen years to qualify for higher positions such as Druid High Priest, and High Priestess.

THE BOY JESUS PREPARED
FOR CORNWALL, ENGLAND

It was this reputation for superior education that led the wealthy Joseph of Arimathea to take his grand nephew the boy Jesus, and his own son Adnam Josephus, at the age of twelve years, to the Glastonbury College of Druidism, where they would gain the best education the world had to offer at that time, and where the boys would be supported and cared for by Joseph's relatives when Joseph was away on his trading vessel.

Joseph and Holy Mary, the parents of Jesus, readily agreed to the plan for the two boys to travel to Britain. The parents motives being the anxiety to get Jesus and Adnam away from Judea where no one was entirely safe from murder, blackmail, or abuse from the occupying Romans. Joseph and Holy Mary were comforted by the knowledge that the relatives of the wealthy and influential Joseph of Arimathea would care for the youngsters. Added to which Joseph would be visiting the boys frequently on his regular round trips from Joppa in Judea to Britain, when the boys could exchange letters to their mothers, and family in Judea.

In Judea it was the time of Passover in the Jewish calendar. In preparation for the trip to Britain, Joseph and Holy Mary took Jesus up to the Temple in Jerusalem to ask the Temple Priests for a special blessing for his journey. Joseph of Arimathea, himself a Temple Priest, had taken Jesus regularly to the Temple for religious instruction on special Temple days. It was on those occasions that Joseph and the other Temple Priests discovered that Jesus was probably a child genius, and must be afforded the best education the world had to offer.

Jesus was at home in the Temple and stayed at the Temple all day, a place to which he referred as 'God's House'.

Jesus also loved the Temple Priests who in return loved him dearly. (The same priests who, in the future, would be calling for his execution). Jesus could barely contain his excitement and tears as he called back to the Priests waving "MY SPECIAL JOURNEY BEGINS, AND MY GOD WILL BE WITH ME ALL THE WAY". The Temple Priests shed tears of love as they saw Jesus running down the Temple steps, trying to catch up to his parents who had scolded him for being too long at the Temple. When Jesus arrived at his home, He being the eldest, made his farewells to his brothers and sisters, the next eldest being James. Jesus promised to send presents from Britain and letters explaining the way of life there.

Joseph of Arimathea arrived with Adnam to collect Jesus and his belongings. Joseph explained to the whole family that his relatives owned tin smelters near Glastonbury in Britain, and would house and care for the boys. The relatives would teach the boys about mining and smelting, and trading ferrous and non-ferrous metals, essential to the Romans. That the boys would attend the Druid College of Learning and when they returned to Judea, would be wiser and more educated than himself, and would be ready to join the family business.

MASTER MARINER
JOSEPH OF ARIMATHEA

Joachim and Ann were the father and mother to Holy Mary. Joseph of Arimathea was the younger brother by five years to Joachim, making him a relative to Jesus, usually referred to as the great uncle of Jesus. Joachim's family were part owners of a trading vessel that sailed from the Port of Joppa in Judea. Joachim sent his brother Joseph, to live on the Island of Rhodes, to act as the family's Shipping Agent, and to learn more about the business before he was sent to sea with the vessel to qualify as a Master Mariner.

It was on the Island of Rhodes that Joseph met and worked with a ship owner, who fathered only daughters. Joseph fell in love with and married the eldest daughter, foregoing the traditional lengthy courtship, much to the delight of the ship owner, who was very fond of Joseph because of his honesty and devotion to religion. He took Joseph under his wing, but while Joseph was away sailing with the fast trader, the owner, his father-in-law, died suddenly after a short illness.

On Joseph's return to port, the deceased's wife (his mother-in-law), and family, asked Joseph to take over the running of the ship and control of the family business, which comprised of buying, selling, bartering luxury goods, and ferrous and non-ferrous metals and ores essential to the Roman war machine. Their trade route ran from Joppa to Cyprus to Rhodes, Greece onto Italy, France, round the straits into Spain and across to the West Coast of Britain. They also carried passengers, to and from the famous ports.

FIRST PORT CYPRUS

Jesus stayed overnight with Adnam Josephus at the Port of Joppa where their vessel was being prepared for the sea journey. The two boys boarded the ship at first light on the following morning. Jesus was wide eyed as he saw the ship making ready to sail. A few Phoenician passengers were boarding to travel to the Port of Citium in Cyprus where the ship would dock. Rested after the Jewish holiday, carpenters loaded down with their tools, boarded the ship to return to work on the Island of Rhodes.

The last of the cargo being manhandled across the gangplank comprised the more valuable luxury goods, whilst at the same time heavy crates were being winched aboard by rope and pulley. The boys could not believe the variety of cargo before their eyes, rolls of silk and crates containing pottery packed in straw. The last of the jars of spices, plus barrels of soap made from olives, were being loaded into the forward hold. The more valuable items such as vessels of beaten silver, bags of gold grain, and nodules of myrrh from Africa, were being carried to the Captain's cabin. Joseph, himself, sported a bag of precious stones around his neck, bought and bartered from the Jewellers in Tyre, a major Phoenician seaport, just north of Jerusalem, founded in the 15th century B.C. Last to be taken to the Captain's quarters were piles of brightly coloured clothes, soft leather shoes and sandals.

Polished marble slabs would be taken on board for transportation to Rome, where they would be used for building Roman bathhouses, the envy of the world. Drinking cups would be purchased to satisfy demand at every port on the trade route to Britain. Jars of olives were a popular food commodity. They could be sold in measured quantities at ports from the large jars, always carried on board. The first working task allocated to the boys when they docked at Cyprus was to measure out the olives and take payment. They were, however, unable to deal with all the barter offered in exchange for whole jars of olives. Grand Uncle Joseph would step in to help and advise, but leave the boys to conclude deals. Grand Uncle Joseph promised Jesus and Adnam a feast of a lifetime on goat's cheese and pickled birds, a favourite food of the Italians, to be loaded on board in barrels when they reached Cyprus, and a delicacy that would stand in storage for up to a year.

The island of Rhodes was the next important port of call. Rhodes was the home of ship building and ship repairs for much of the Middle-East.

Joseph's vessel stopped only long enough to give the skipper sufficient time to take on board important parts and spares necessary to a sailing vessel that was going to spend many weeks at sea. Also to disembark sail makers and carpenters with their families returning to work and business. After which, with no more delay, the skipper got quickly underway.

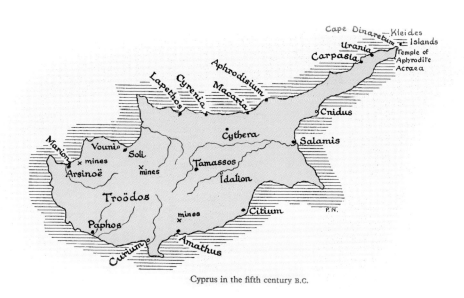

Cyprus in the fifth century B.C.

Their sailing ship arrived at the Port of Athens just after dawn. Eager to venture ashore, the boys rose early and were fully awake. Joseph warned Jesus and Adnam that Athens Port was a massive trading centre, and not necessarily safe, and that the boys must stay together at all times.

Nothing could have prepared the boys for the hustle and bustle they encountered as soon as they left the gang plank. Traders came from as far away as the Black Sea Ports to trade their wheat for olive oil. Joseph caught up with the boys as they wondered along the quayside. Joseph wanted to introduce the boys to important Phoenician merchants with whom he did business.

The merchants had just arrived from Carthage. Their servants carried rolls of bright purple cloth, their speciality, which Joseph needed to purchase for the Druids in England and the tailors in Rome. Ever curious, the boys asked the Phoenicians how they achieved such a vivid purple colour in their cloth. Surprisingly, perhaps, the merchants were eager to explain the gruesome story of how they extracted the sought after dye. The boys listened intently, and enjoyed every moment of the described procedure.

The older merchant explained that the dye came from a mollusc named Murez, a mollusc that lived in waters all around the Mediterranean coastline. The molluscs were collected from the seawater, heaped into piles and left to die. Eventually a purple liquid oozed from the piles. This was collected and the shells were left to dry in the strong sunshine, after which they were carved into jewellery or made into many forms of wall decorations.

The merchants explained to the boys that they were always on the move. After one area was emptied of Murez, they needed to travel on to find new beds of molluscs. While they were away from home their wives took advantage of their absence to use the time to dye wool and cloth. However, the merchants always returned with the finished products to the same trading centres. All of which sold very quickly, such was the demand for the purple coloured cloth.

After their discussions had ended, Joseph struck a deal with the merchants to buy all the material on offer, bartering gold, silk, and some food products such as olives, pickled birds, and fish, all contained in barrels. A very successful day.

ITALY
SERMIONI PENINSULAR

After setting sail from Greece, Joseph's ship crossed the Aegean Sea, wide berthing Greek islands, dangerous because of the pirates operating off the coast of Greece. The next port of call was the Italian Sermioni Peninsular where there was a large Roman store and workshop eager to buy the copper ore from Cyprus loaded on board, and some of the food delicacies and dried fruit.

Close to the shore, the boys observed bubbles of sulpher rising from the sea floor. A smell of bad eggs was all around. Joseph explained to the boy that the smell was due to volcanic activity on the sea bed. This stop amounted to only a short sojourn before sailing for Rome and great opportunities for trade.

MARSEILLES

When the boys went ashore in Marseilles, they were immediately captured by the variety of smells ranging from perfume to dung. The many colours of the dyed felts on rolls of fabric in the Quayside tents were dazzling. The boys were amazed at the assortment and variety of boots carried on the shoulders of cobblers who pestered them along the way. The people appeared happy, and the sellers could barter in many languages. Even the beggars who cried their crocodile tears for alms, called out in different languages. Jesus said to Adnam, there are beggars in every port, and they will always be with us.

Wood turners stamped away on the pedals driving their lathes, turning out bowls and selling almost immediately, as they were taken from the lathe. Roadside potters barely had time to dry their clay pots before they were bought and loaded onto carts. Joseph could never obtain sufficient Myrrh (perfumed resin from African Burseraceous trees fetched up from Africa to

Egypt) or Frankincense, to satisfy demand from French makers of perfumers and perfumed incense sticks.

Gold grain brought up from Africa by the Myrrh traders always commanded good prices in both Rome and Marseilles. It was truly a case of rationing out these precious commodities to keep the port merchants happy until the next shipment. If Joseph found the supplies he needed were in short supply, he would travel along the river Rhone to Lyons to fulfil many orders for the journey to England.

ROME

During the leg of the journey to Rome, Joseph explained to the boys that Rome sucked in all the wealth of the Mediterranean countries for itself, using force of mass genocide and slavery, when it suited their needs. Rome itself was a pagan, violent, uncaring society. A Senate controlled the wealth of the Roman Empire, mostly for its own benefit. Nevertheless, it was a City that offered great opportunities for trade. Many Romans lived in apartments above their business workshops in the port areas and developed an insatiable appetite for luxury goods and cloths from the Middle East.

Beyond these apartments lay the outskirts of the City which was a hotbed of crime and literal filth and disease. The Senate forestalled unrest in these deprived areas with regular handouts of wheat and bread. The boys were prohibited from venturing to those areas. The demand from the Port Traders in Rome would be for sugar, pepper, spices, linen, muslin, silks, dyes and jewels. Joseph said he would be looking to barter or buy homespun dyed linen and wool cloths. Hoping to buy the finest cloths available in Rome for his customers in Marseilles and Britain, such as Kings and high ranking Druids.

Joseph also explained to Jesus and Adnam that he would be expected to buy as much wool and woven woollen blankets in Britain as he could load on board to sell and barter at the Port of Rome on his return journey, however, priority of allocation of space would be given to carrying ferrous and non-ferrous metal ingots from his relatives' smelters and businesses in Britain, which would produce a higher profit return than wool.

After rounding the Straits and heading towards Spain, the sea became very rough with high waves pounding the side of the ship. Jesus, who we must remember was only twelve, called out to Grand Uncle Joseph, "Give me a length of ship's rope and I will calm the storm". The amused Joseph, a man of great patience, gave Jesus a length of ship's rope. Jesus proceeded to tie three knots. "Look what my God will do", he called to Joseph. Jesus untied the first knot and the wind dropped almost immediately. Jesus untied the second knot in the rope, and the sea calmed. The astonished and shocked Joseph and Adnam stared at Jesus, who said, "I will not untie the third knot unless I call on God to save our very souls".

Joseph knew from that moment what he felt about Jesus, was confirmed beyond any doubt. Jesus was someone very very special who unwittingly revealed that he could perform miracles, and that he, Joseph, had made the right decision to take Jesus to the high Druids in Britain for a very special education, to prepare him fully for whatever destiny lay ahead of him. Joseph also knew the rest of the journey would be safe. Joseph also called to mind the mental picture of Jesus running down the steps from the Temple in Jerusalem, and calling back to the Temple Priests "My journey has begun, and my God will be with me all the way".

TARSHISH
A SPANISH PORT

Whilst docking at Tarshish, a pretty but busy Spanish port, Joseph spotted that a Middle East trader had arrived before them, which might mean that selling opportunities could be limited. Disembarking for shore, Jesus was surprised that grand uncle was so well known. The Spanish people were friendly, happy, and it was safe for the boys to venture and explore before returning to the ship later in the day.

The boys were surprised to see that Joseph had indeed been very successful, for they could see Greek wine, lathe turned marble cups and bowls, which had been taken on board in Cyprus, silks and fine cloths being off loaded onto the dockside, whilst silver bars and jewellery, beaten silver plates, and chalices were being taken on board and straight to the Captain's cabin. The last of the passengers, craftsmen with their families, left the ship, and the vessel put to sea before sunset, heading out to sea and into the Westerly winds that would drive their vessel across to Britain.

Three days out to sea, Jesus and Adnam were astonished to see their ship being overtaken by a fast Roman trading vessel, packed with Roman soldiers, all waving madly and calling out, although their voices were lost in the wind. Joseph explained to the boys that the Roman vessel was heading to Britain to disembark new recruits at St. Michael's Mount; to embark soldiers returning to Rome, together with collecting metal ingots bought from his relatives' smelters in Western Britain. However, having spotted Joseph's vessel on route, the Roman vessel may decide to leave the metal ingots for Joseph to transport to Rome allowing them a faster turnaround. Joseph's family held the exulted appointment as Minister of Mines to Rome and were allowed to use the Imperial Roman Stamp on their ingots.

To prepare them for their life in England, Joseph scheduled the boys' periods of study on most days of the week during their journey, with the exception of the Sabbath, or special days listed in the Jerusalem Temple calendar. Joseph explained to Jesus and Adnam that most of the people they would meet in the areas where they would be working and studying, spoke the Celtic language, which was rarely written. He told the boys it was incumbent upon them to learn this language from his notes. There would be oral practice each free day. Joseph went on to explain that Glastonbury was a village of foreign traders.

There were many languages used, but it would be advisable to pick up an understanding of as many words as possible as they went on their travels. They would come across small markets close to villages where there would be a bedlam of languages and dialects used, often beyond his comprehension. It was a small miracle that everyone selling or buying goods in these markets were able to make themselves understood, but understand each other, they did. Like all children of their age, languages became no problem and they were soon masters of many.

ARRIVING

IN

ENGLAND

ILS Mount, antiently call'd by the Cornish Men Cara tonz, in tOWze, but antienter Dynsol, has on its top an antient
igious House. Wm E. of Cornwall & Moriton, Nephew to Wm y Cong.r built y Monastery & annex'd it as a Cell to the larger
astery of St Mich de Periculo Maris in Normandy. Till K.R.1st time y Mount seems to have serv'd for Religion only, but
de la Pomeroy of Bery Pomeroy Castle in Devonsh having kill'd a Serj' at Arms of y K. who was sent to take him in Custa
new to y Mount, surpriz'd it. expulsed y Monks & fortify'd y Rocky Sides of it In° tore E. of Oxon. after y defeat of K.Hen 6 at
rnesfield. came to y Place by Shining, disguis'd himself nh some of his followers in Pilgrims Habits, thereby got entrance. mas
y Garrison & seiz'd y Place nh he valliantly defended for a long time against y Power of K.Ed 4th but was at last oblig'd to sur
er. In y 13 of K.H.7th y Lady Catherine Gordon Wife of Perkin Warbeck, fled here for Safety, but was soon taken Prisoner by
Ld Doulney & brought to y K. In K.Ed 5. time, during y Cornish Commotion y Place was taken & plunder'd by y Rebels. In the
Civil Wars K. Ch.1st confin'd Duke Hamilton here, but y Parham' Forces besieg'd it. took it & releas'd y Duke. About 150 Yrs
. as they were digging at y bottom of y Mountain for Tin, they met wth Spear Heads. Axes & Swords of Brass all wrap'd
in Linnen. As y Sea stones or ebbs. it is alternately either Island. or joynd to y Main Land by a large Beach of Sand and
les. The present worthy Possessor of it. hath built at y foot of the Mount. a Noble & Capacious Peer. or Mole. where a great
mber of Ships. may in all Safety. be laid up. Clean'd and Refitted.

Sam.l Nath.l Buck. del. it sculp.t 175

At first light the lookout on Joseph's ship called out that he had sighted the West coast of England through the mist. Joseph immediately summoned the boys to explain to them that when the ship docked, activity on board would be frantic. They needed to concentrate their minds on what was happening. Offloading must be carried out with precision because of the large numbers and variety of commodities on board, many of which would be dispatched in different directions. Care must be taken to ensure that the cargo was offloaded onto the correct vessel. The responsibility of the boys would be to carry the more fragile and valuable items from the Captain's Cabin to the correct vessel.

Joseph explained that the first goods to be offloaded were those destined for a smaller sailing vessel, called a 'Tin' ship. Both he and the boys would later be transferring onto this smaller sailing vessel. All the cargo would then be transferred into the open hold on a barge. The barge would make its way inland along the inland waterways to supply a network of relatives and regular customers who would be eagerly awaiting the goods to restock their shops and market stalls. Much of the trade from the barge would be bartered in exchange for metal ingots, so that the barge would eventually return, fully loaded to their own vessel for the outward journey. The whole business would be conducted by relatives of Joseph's family.

Joseph went on to explain that their smaller sailing vessel, would sail round the headland point into an inland waterway, which was tidal.

They would wait on the fast running tide which would take them inland direct to the Isle of Avalon where there was a jetty and landing stage where they would offload the tin ship. Relatives, cousins, and customers would be waiting to cheer their vessel home. Shopkeepers, traders, and jewellery makers would, themselves, collect goods from the landing stage. Joseph also explained to Jesus and Adnam that, in England, people would address him as Joseph of Avalon, and usually treated him with honour and great respect.

When all the work was done, Joseph told the boys that he would take them on a journey around the area to meet members of his extended family, both to introduce them, and to distribute the gifts they had brought with them and also to show the boys where they would be staying. Joseph also wanted the boys to understand that he needed all the ingots smelted in the area, to maintain his prestigious position as a Minister of Mines for Rome. This gave him influence and importance to Romans at the highest level which, in turn, ensured him and his relatives, freedom from meddling by the interfering nearest Roman Garrison. Joseph emphasized that because of the importance of metals to the Roman war machine, the Romans kept a very low profile in districts where ore was mined and smelted.

One unusual job for the boys would be delivering to the relatives' smelters the marble cup, chalices and bowls carved on foot peddle lathes. The smelters would soak these marble items in honey, after which they would be heated to bring out the beautiful patterns and lines in the marble. Finished in this way, the marble pieces would fetch good prices in gold and silver from the King. Small marble panels would also be given this same treatment and fashioned into boxes by local jewellers.

The final trip on the agenda would be to take the boys to the Druid school where they would be students for the next 10-15 years. They would take along with them rolls of cloth and other items to pay for their education in the first year of study under their Druid teachers. Joseph revealed that he owned five hides of land, comprising the Isle of Avalon, land given to him by the local King in consideration of the importance to the King of all the business Joseph brought to the area on every return journey.

CORNISH MINERS

Miners in Cornwall worked in dangerous conditions, climbing down holes in the ground and crawling along dark crevices lit only by small Roman style oil lamps. The light from their lamps was nevertheless, sufficient to reflect off the bright spots in the rock holding the tin ore. Miners would then bore into the rock using a hammer head in either hand, boring preferably upwards, by doing this the bore holes would be self cleaning.

Very early miners used antlers tied to a handle to use as picks. Luck played a big part in miners' fortunes, because a load could be as small as a few kilos or a wedge of tin ore or silver weighing several tonnes, occasionally embedded in soft rock that enabled the wedge to be pulled from the walls or ceiling with ropes.

With the availability of coal from what is now known as Wales and wood from forests in the Mendip Hills, smelters were able to reach temperatures required for winning the ore from its rock and then pouring into moulds to produce ingots. Also melting iron ore and casting into clay moulds.

Green malachite (copper ore) went through the same treatment. Bronze was very hard and water resistant. Gained from smelting copper and smaller proportions of tin, zinc and lead. The process that lent its name to the 'Bronze Age' three thousand years earlier.

Joseph Arrives at a Cornish Cove to Collect Ingots of Silver and Tin

After their first evening meal in their new home, the boys chatted excitedly, discussing a plan to ask Joseph if they could help him build a traditional Jewish Meeting House, in the oblong shape that would accommodate a group of visitors. They felt they could work on such a project after returning from school at the end of the day, and during the weekly break.

Before falling asleep Adnam confessed to Jesus that he could not conceive how ten or fifteen years would pass before they finished their schooling. It seemed to Adnam an impossible number of years even to contemplate. "Be of good cheer", replied Jesus. "Our God will be with us throughout our time here".

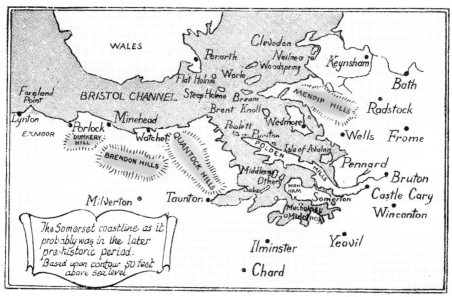

Drawn by Eustace Nash

When Jesus arrived at Glastonbury Lake Villages, he was amazed to see, for the first time, circular huts about 20ft in diameter, built on a log base with a thatched roof and wattle-and-daub walls. Inside the walls was a circular fire hearth for cooking, heating water for ablutions and washing clothes. The smoke from the fire passed through windows with wooden shutters or cloth blinds fixed on the outside walls.

Standing on the log floor close to the outside wall were clay pitchers of water. Hanging on the walls were leather bottles and carved wooden spoons for eating. Below were wooden platters and bowls. Inside the bowls were thin oblong stirring spoons, made from horn. There were two wooden beds, each had a woollen rug for a mattress, and a woven wool blanket. There were two reed baskets standing next to the wall holding linen towels. Two shirts and under trousers were also hanging from a wooden peg. Between the beds stood a table with three chairs. On the table were a linen cloth and a freshly baked loaf of black bread. A clay pot decorated with circles and cross stitch contained delicious honey still in the honeycomb.

For the evening meal, a black metal pot hung over the centre fire hearth. In the hearth there was a clay plate full of smoked herring. There were several small clay oil lamps and a pot of oil to light the room when darkness fell. Jesus and Adnam commented to Joseph, that whilst quite different in shape and structure from the houses in which they lived in Judea, they felt comfortable. A cosy place from which to leave early every morning to walk to the Druid School. Joseph told the boys that when they returned in the evening, their only tasks were to fetch drinking water from a choice of well or spring, also digging their own rubbish pit when the pit in use was full.

THE DRUID SCHOOL

The Druid School comprised around 40 circular huts. The teaching school was at the centre, contained within a round hut about 45 feet in diameter which was used in the Cold Period, traditionally from 1st November. The warm period commenced on 1st May, when schooling would be held in the open air. The Cold

Period of schooling lasted from 1st November to 1st February. The Warm Period of school lasted from 1st May to 1st August after which school finished until the start of the Cold Period on 1st November.

Most traders lived a short walking distance from the Druid Cor, within a close knit village community of around a hundred circular huts. Druid Priests, teachers and students did not venture out from their community. The exception was the occasions when Druids were summoned by villagers to attend the sick. Typically to dispense medicines, use trance hypnosis, or perform the Ceremony of Casting out Demons into animals. On the occasions when all the treatments failed to illicit any improvement in the patient, the patient would be carried on a litter to a Sacred Grove for a full Ceremony of healing.

THE SCHOOL DAY

The following day Joseph arrived at the boys dwelling before they were ready to leave for school. Joseph waited patiently to accompany them to their Druid teachers, who would show them the robes they would be wearing at the school. Joseph also explained that the area, in which they now lived and worked, would normally enjoy warm summer months and mild winters. They would discover Palm and Yucca growing in the climate, also plants very similar to the areas around Marseille. In the winter though, the heavy winds coming into the coast made it impossible to sail.

Joseph went on to explain that school was intense, but lasted only two to three days each session, because all teaching had to be committed to memory. Free time would be taken up visiting the relatives who ran the tin mines and smelters in a wide circle around the area. The trips inland would be made mostly by boat along rivers that criss-cross the whole region and co-joined at important trading centres. The boys would be rowing most of the way which would be good for building their personal strength. Longer trips would be made further inland to barter their store of luxury goods and essentials, in exchange for copper ingots and ingots of lead which would be deposited at trading points for collection later.

Joseph also told the two students that he would keep a watchful eye to spot traders from a large Island off the West Coast of Britain who would fetch gold in exchange for luxury items. These traders could be recognised by their distinctive rhythmical mother tongue, but these peoples had no language skills themselves. Joseph said he was, however, well known to them as a trader of all manner of barter goods. Occasionally trips would be made even further inland to meet small dark skinned peoples who would barter heavy loads of iron ingots about one metre in length weighing 80 kilos. These heavy ingots would be packed into boats hewn from logs. These log boats were very stable and could be towed easily by rowers on high or low tides.

Bronze Age Logistics

Long before the Romans arrived with their road building skills, the rivers in Cornwall and Somerset were ready made natural highways essential to the miners and smelters for the transportation of its heavy loads to trading points inland and to the coastal ports.

Long flat-bottomed log boats hewn from a single tree were reliable in carrying a goodly load at a moderate pace to their destination. The long history of this system of transportation for moving metals along the rivers dates back thousands of years to the Bronze Age.

Not only were these small boats connected by the many rivers extending to the Cornish Coast, but routes also ran through to the North Channel in the West.

Pilton Harbour in Somerset became a main trading post to which the tinners, lead and silver makers, brought their ingots for weighing, barter and sale. Pilton was used extensively by Joseph of Arimathea and his team to assemble loads along the route from the Mendip Plateau down to the coast. At Pilton, ingots were stored in a small wattle and daub Meeting House built by Joseph and his band to accommodate the party during the sometimes, long wait through the Winter months.

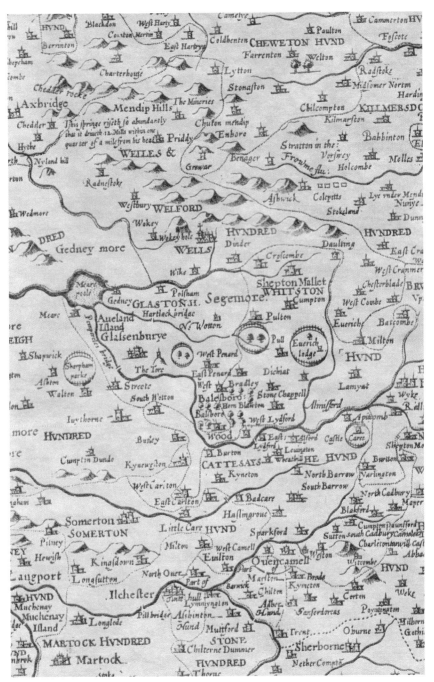

Ancient Map in the Possession of the Rayner Family

Joseph told the boys that some of the villagers would venture out from the village to consult a Celtic Shaman for the casting of spells, and healing by magic. These magicians must be avoided at all costs, for they are connected to evil and evil deeds that are far from our God. Go not near them or by them, and do not listen to their supposed deeds for they worship the Sun God. You will recognise them from the painting of the skin, their blue wild hair, plus bells and other items hanging from their clothes. It is rumoured that these magicians are involved in human sacrifices.

Jesus and Adnam returned to their roundhouse dwelling after their first day with their Druid teachers. Sitting at the table enjoying their evening meal of warm pottage, herrings and fruit, Jesus spoke to Adnam at his surprise at being told by their teacher that everything they were taught had to be committed to memory. Adnam replied that he felt it was a strange rule, more particularly because in their classes at the Temple in Jerusalem, most of what they were taught was copied down on to parchment for the benefit of returning to the subject being taught for revision. Jesus said he was surprised that the teacher placed such importance on this rule to the point of being adamant that there will be no deviation tolerated. Nothing of Druid teachings are to be written on parchment or carved into wood.

Adnam recounted the teachers' words. "Everything you learn over the many years stay at this school, will leave this school recorded into your memory and never to be forgotten. It is not for those outside this school to know any knowledge of our many secrets and methods, or for anyone who is not a Druid Priest to teach others our ways". Jesus told Adnam that when he asked the teacher why these rules were introduced, the teacher explained that almost every student attending the Cor came from different parts of the world outside. It would be quite impossible, and take too long in time to teach all students to scribe in Anglo Roman or Anglo Saxon.

Later in the evening as the boys lay in their beds, Jesus commented to Adnam, that such was the closeness of the Druid Religion to their own Jewish Religion, he felt he was learning some of their own Jewish principles for a second time. "I wonder Adnam, that if the Druid Priests do not relent on their rule prohibiting record keeping, this wonderful Garden of Eden will fade away". "One interesting matter our teacher taught today", replied Adnam "is his belief that earth is of its own domain. Created by our God, but acts of itself, acting in its own timeless existence just like a living cell". "Druids understand this principle" said the teacher, "but other men in their vanity do not". "Only Druids and farmers understand that when men work with and respect trees, plants, and animals, a great bounty will be mans for the taking. Damage or poison the earth", said the teacher, "and earth will bring about the conditions that will wipe away mankind in proportion to the damage he has done. Man must not blame God if earth bound catastrophes wipe away man, for our God's domain is the domain of mankind".

CURING THE SICK

Jesus called across to Adnam. We will cure many people in our homeland with our knowledge and practice of making medicines from herbs. Also the paste for treating and soothing skin, laying on of our hands, trancing with poetry, followed by prayer, will heal all manner of mental and emotional pain. What a wonderful adventure for the two of us Adnam. Let us rejoice in our heart and mind and be glad, for we are part of God's plan.

God spoke to me in a dream Adnam. He told me that he will give us the power to heal. But the first step for those seeking our cures, is to forgive their sins, for sin blocks channels through which cures work. Those who have ears to hear must repent their sins through prayer, or their malady may return seven fold. These are powerful words from God Adnam. Hearing His Words, or reading His Words with repentance and prayer will bring about a cure.

"I have a surprise for you Adnam, a present, I have constructed a poem for our teacher tomorrow, and I would like you to hear the words before I read them to all the students".

There is no death
Our Spirit will never die
We will take a step forward in the twinkling of an eye

As we enter our next life all memories are left behind
All gone in an instant of time

Through the portal we shall reap only what we have sown
Unable to lie and place on others responsibility for our sins

The Good shall go on to paths of righteousness
Sinners will go on to a future far worse than that from whence they came
Not for the sinner will be the higher plane

But our God is forever
Time and Eternity shall be His name
To reign supreme above all that there is
Send His Holy Spirit to His Faithful on Earth to
Guide us and Help us and ease our Pain

Adnam loved the poem. "It is certain that our teacher will be pleased". Jesus replied. "You had said yesterday Adnam you did not feel you could bear so many long years at this place, but would do so to show your father, Joseph, your love and your faith. I tell you Adnam, this place is God's plan for us, and we should rejoice and be glad in every working day. We must not pine for our homeland, for here we are doing God's work every day, until the light of the day fades away".

At that moment, there was a loud knock and Joseph appeared at the door.

THE DRUID URIM AND THUMMIN

The next day, Jesus and Adnam were surprised when they arrived at school to find Joseph seated in the centre of a circle of High Priests.

All eyes gazing at Joseph who was untying a leather thong around his neck on which hung a small fine purse. Joseph emptied the contents carefully upon the table before him, revealing a number of sparkling coloured gemstones. Joseph looked up at the Priests who gazed in amazement and total silence at the gemstones. This is my gift to you said Joseph, for caring for the boys during my absence. You must set these stones into a gold breastplate.

The religion of the Prophets, name such a breastplate - The Urim and Thummin. In addition to scrying with your crystals, a breastplate of gold, and precious gems, will enable you to scry into the future. However, before you set out on this course, be aware that you may see future events of a nature that you do not wish to see. Nevertheless, a warning enables everyone to make preparations ahead of bad events coming upon you. In my experience Scrying also reveals the How of God and the Why of God.

The only First Century portrait of Jesus

27

THE FIRST VISION OF
THE BOY JESUS

Later that day all three returned to the round hut. When they were seated, Jesus told Joseph "when I was scrying with my Druid teacher, I enjoyed a vision, Great Uncle Joseph, I saw God as a wave of unimaginable beauty. A voice spoke to me":

"MY SPIRIT IS FOR ALL THE PEOPLES OF THE EARTH

THERE IS NO RACE OR TRIBE IN MY HEART THAT IS ABOVE
ANOTHER IN MY KINGDOM

THOSE WHO ARE CLEAN AND GOOD AND OBEY MY
COMMANDMENTS

MY SPIRIT WILL GO WITH THEM ALWAYS IN THIS LIFE AND INTO
THE NEXT

MY SPIRIT WILL BE FOR TIME AND ETERNITY

THOSE WHO CALL UPON MY SPIRIT IN PRAYER SHALL BE SAVED

THOSE WHO DO NOT LOVE ME OR OBEY MY COMMANDMENTS,

OR REPENT THEIR SINS

WILL KNOW IN THEIR HEARTS THAT THEY ARE NOT OF MY PLAN

FOR HUMAN KIND

AND WILL PASS AWAY INTO THE ETERNAL DARKNESS.

THEY HAVE CHOSEN THEIR WAY"

"GREAT TRAVAIL WILL COME UPON HUMANKIND WHO ARE NOT
OF MY WORLD

THEY HAVE RETURNED TO THE ANIMAL FROM WHICH I LIFTED
THEM UP

MY EARTH WILL CLEAN ITS FABRIC OF THOSE EVIL ONES WITH

GREAT FLOODING, BURNING, PESTILENCE AND FAMINE

GREAT TROUBLES THEY HAVE NEVER BEFORE SEEN

THE SINNERS SHALL BE NO MORE, AND THE FABRIC OF THE
EARTH

SHALL BE CLEANSED ONCE MORE"

JESUS AND THE DRUID PRIESTS

Jesus and his cousin remained in Cornwall to continue business while Joseph returned with a fully laden ship via European ports to Israel. The young men were quite safe, as Joseph was one of the few metal merchants authorised to use the Roman Imperial Stamp on ingots at the smelters. Everyone was aware that Jesus and his cousin could bring the much-feared Roman soldiers from the small Cornwall Garrison if they ran into any serious problems.

Joseph of Arimathea was well known and respected in the areas surrounding the smelters as an authority on the Jewish Law and he became a sought after speaker throughout the area. Joseph's travels gave Jesus and his cousin the opportunity to meet with all the tribal priests and leaders of the Druid communities and to study the practices and customs of their holy men. This included their methods for healing and casting out devils, which involved much ceremony, the daubing of blue paint (wode) and the ingredients and preparations of potions that could take away feeling and pain after a serious injury.

The local Druids regarded Joseph of Arimathea as an exulted teacher from a land far off, which they knew to be the land of the great prophets. The Chief Druid went to Joseph's camp, with the message that it was clear to the local Druid Priests that Joseph was also a man of their One God; a Prophet and teacher revered by your own people.

You are a teacher to your student Jesus who shows undoubted unique and outstanding qualities for a youth of his age. Forever questioning the Druid Priests and Priestesses about their philosophy and teachings; acquainting them with the teachings of the Prophets in his own lands with knowledge far above his years. The Chief Druid invited Jesus and Adnam to attend a Druid Ceremony to be held on the following day, the day of the full moon, and before Sunset.

Joseph had returned from his ship with much to tell the boys. It was late in the afternoon when the trio arrived at the appointed place at which Druid Ceremonies were held locally. The location of the ceremony was in the opening of a cave surrounded by oak trees. It was clear that a ceremony was under way. A Chief Priest stood in the centre of the cave entrance behind a large white stone, close to a second stone hollowed into, containing rainwater.

In front of this stone was a fire where burnt offerings were placed around the head of a bull. In front of the burnt offerings sat a Priest with the skin of a bull draped around his shoulders reciting poetry, followed by a prayer to the One God.

The Chief Priest was standing behind the main stone adorned in a coloured robe. Priests and Priestesses stood on either side in white robes. After a brief ceremony, the Head Priest beckoned Joseph to come forward and the two sat together inside the cave entrance.

The Head Priest explained to Joseph that he was aware that he, Joseph, was a wealthy and worthy man, and could afford to pay for the long training that would be necessary for his student Jesus to train to become a Druid Priest – seeker of truth, healer and teacher. Prolonged training was necessary because everything Druids' taught was learned in their heart and committed to memory. Every detail concerning the sacred duties to be undertaken by Druid Priests had to be committed to memory.

The Head Priest confided in Joseph the views of both himself and other priests who met Jesus and Adnam; that Jesus was destined to reach the exulted position of Arch Druid, long before ten summers had passed, because everything about Jesus was in praise of the One God and the Reincarnation. Adnam was also destined for the position of Arch Druid.

ROMAN LIES ABOUT DRUIDS

Many Druids were tall, moustached, educated, civilised, trustworthy in trade, men of great skill and strength. Britain was a manufacturing centre for metals and other goods of world renown. This truthful cameo of ancient Britains is far removed from the many lies and propaganda of the Roman historians, and even our own early historians.

In very truth it was the Romans who were the barbarians from the most barbarous nation in the whole of Europe. The Romans lacked the knowledge or sense of moral right and wrong, never mastering the skills of the peoples they conquered. The Romans in reality were an inferior race of organised warmongers who plundered, slaughtered, and slaved; leaving a nasty stain on almost every country they conquered.

Romans left nothing of any real value in their wake, except heathen monuments to the extreme vanity of their leaders. Gods that could only have been dreamt up by the minds of those who enjoyed the ridiculous and sick spectacle of inhuman slaughter of slaves and animals in arenas for the enjoyment of their bloodthirsty masses. A very different picture to the Druidic communities in Britain who they destroyed in their familiar bloody revengeful acts of wanton murder and slaughter.

Jesus was well aware that he was a descendant of the Royal line of David, a Priest King. As he grew older, following in the footsteps of Joseph of Arimathea, Jesus himself became an authority on Jewish Law with a knowledge and understanding far in advance of his years. During Joseph's absence for many months during his return trips to the Far East, Jesus filled in as a speaker, travelling far and wide in the area learning as much as possible about local customs and belief systems.

In the sixteen years the trio spent in Cornwall they built a second Meeting House and became favourites of the Jewish community throughout the area. Such was their popularity they built their own wattle and daub Meeting House on Glastonbury Tor, alongside the Druid Temple. Joseph, Jesus and Joseph's son were all regarded by the Druids as holy men, worshipping the same God, who provided goods and work for the local population. They also had customs in common, such as Baptism, and burnt offerings.

News of the Druids' Cornish success in mining and smelting Tin, Copper, Lead, Silver and Iron plus the valuable products from their fishing industry, already well known by the Romans, spread throughout Britain and across to Europe. Many more ships from ports in the South of Britain and from Gaul arrived in the Cornish ports to barter and trade. Some of the European crews were unscrupulous, and did not maintain the high standards set by the Jews.

After travelling and trading in Cornwall and Europe successfully for sixteen years the trio decided the time was right to return to Israel where they would be safer until the Roman Garrison in Cornwall had brought about some order to the mining areas.

Jesus looked forward to returning to Palestine in Spring, seeing the mass colour of Palestine in Bloom – crimson, pale blue, lilac, yellow, cream, purple and pink. Longing also to see his extended family once more to which he would most probably give the appearance of a fully matured Rabbi. Jesus knew that having been away for such a long period of time and gained so much knowledge, he was in danger of appearing as a perfect stranger to his own family. Nevertheless, Jesus was longing to reveal to the fishermen of Galilee the skills he had learned in Cornwall, included new ways of netting fish; different methods of preparation and storing of fish, plus the oils that were the result of processing fish.

Jesus was also enthusiastic about visiting and speaking at the Meeting Houses in Galilee, and to see how they had grown in number. Jesus learnt much from the Druids about the casting out of evil, which was not known, in his own land, and he looked forward to using this gift in Galilee.

THE GENIUS OF JESUS

Jesus saw the vision that the one God was not the domain of the Jews alone, but that the one God was the God of all Gentiles, and Jews alike. Jesus knew he had the mission to take these messages back to Judea; the Good News for everyone.

Jesus knew also that spreading this wondrous news throughout Judea was not possible by one man alone. However, God had given him the wealth to recruit Disciples to build Meeting Houses and devote their lives to spreading God's word. One of the disciples must be a woman to head the women of Galilee. He knew also that when his mission was accomplished, as a descendant of the line of David, he had to go into Jerusalem when the time was right, and in the manner laid down by the Old Testament Prophets, to claim the spiritual kingdom of the Jews as spiritual King.

Joseph of Arimathea told Jesus that if this is the Mission given to you by God, then I will be with you all the way, but you must know Jesus, that the leader of the Jews in the Temple will bay for your blood. They will never understand that the Kingdom you are claiming is the Spiritual Kingdom of the Jews, and not the power to rule over the Sanhedrin. The Kingdom you are claiming is not of this world.

Jesus told Joseph that his Mission is to explain to all mankind that the One God, claimed by the Jews to be The God of the Jews alone, is in fact the God of all mankind. I saw this in a vision as my Mission to spread God's message. The Holy Spirit from the very mind of God will then flow out into the world for the benefit of all mankind, and shall never leave. This spiritual power, direct from God, will wait to be called upon by all who keep God's Commandments. Together with the great gift of eternal life.

JOSEPH AND JESUS LEAVE BRITAIN
TO SAIL FOR ISRAEL

Lead ingots from the Mendip Hills were being loaded into the hold of Joseph's ship. Heavy ingots would act as ballast for the return journey to Joppa, Israel. The smaller tin ship from the Isle of Avalon was behind schedule, usually due to sailing against the strong estuary current under full sail to break out from the estuary to the sea to sail round the point to meet up with Joseph's ship in good time to catch high tide.

In the meantime a barge had arrived from the inland waterways loaded with ingots of copper, silver, and iron. All to be winched up to the deck of Joseph's ship. Joseph commented that the ingots were fewer in number than on the usual loading. The barge Master explained that torrential continuous rainfall in the Mendip Hills rendered the cartways to loading points on overflowing rivers impossible to negotiate, resulting in a reduced amount of ore reaching the Jews Houses for smelting.

The Ship's Master assured Joseph that no hold would remain empty on the return journey to Joppa because there was a goodly supply of woollen blankets and tents for the Army Storemaster in Rome. There were also many barrels of oil and salted fish, also for Rome. Joseph loaded new wooden barrels for transportation to his fishing fleet in Galilee, to experiment with replacing flat sacks used for storing salted fish from the Galilee which Joseph estimated would not preserve as long as salt fish stored in barrels.

All the cargo was stored and lashed with care, because in the early Spring, while the Atlantic had its perils, the Mediterranean Sea had only just opened and could be very rough.

Joseph looked up from an array of parchments and scrolls he was holding to inform the Master Mariner he was pleased, that for the first time, he had on board a collection of rare skins and furs from North Sea Traders, brought to him overland to Glastonbury by salt merchants. Such skins and furs would be in demand at every Port of call on the route home to Joppa for decorating the clothes of the rich.

Last to be loaded were the live oysters in caskets of brine. A profitable delicacy for Rome, sailed round from Rutupiae to Joseph's ship. Then on to Rome where the oysters would still be alive. The Master reminded Joseph that he had reserved room in the hold into which to load wine during a brief stop in Spain.

Their agent will have collected wine from the vineyards along the Dordogne, Lot and Garonne. The wine would be exchanged for ingots of silver needed by the Spanish Silversmiths.

Joseph instructed the Ship's Master. Tell the Silversmiths to reserve for me some fine silver goblets which I will collect on my return journey to Britain. Give them extra ingots from which to make fine goblets but keep a careful tally. Ask them also to make a silver scabbard to fit a Roman Sword. It will be my gift to the Storemaster of the Roman Store at Sermioni.

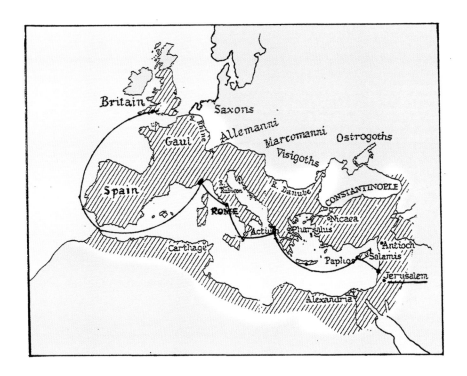

Joseph interrupted his conversation to call to the ship's Master. "If the sky is dark at morning, and there is no sun, use the thunderstone needle to keep the ship away from the rocky shore". "Guard it well. We have only one needle to keep the ship safe from peril. This needle has been used since the time of Moses".

JOSEPHS GRAND PLAN FOR DISCIPLES

Jesus and Joseph both turned to stare at the horizon.

"Your message Jesus, the Good News for all mankind, must be taken to everyone who will listen, not only in our homeland, but to all our Ports of call.

It will be impossible for one man to carry out such a task alone. I have money Jesus, and this is my grand plan. My fishermen on the Galilee are for the most part, the men who minister and run the meeting houses around the lake. They will be your Disciples to travel with you throughout Galilee and down to Judea spreading the Good News, healing the sick and helping the poor. When that task is complete, your Disciples can travel on my ship to all our Ports of business.

Taking the Good News to all those who will listen". "Joseph you are my maker. I pray that I am up to the task". Strolling together to settle for a night's sleep, Joseph said to Jesus, "Tell me Jesus, to what use did the Druids put my gift of twelve precious stones" Jesus replied. "Unlike the Jewish High Priests Joseph, who wore them in a woven pad tied around their chests, the Druids asked the Jews Houses to set the stones in a solid beaten gold plate, made in the shape of the new moon. This was held around the neck of the Druid High Priest with a gold chain".

"What are your thoughts about my son Adnam Josephus staying on the tin island after his appointment as High Priest to the King?"

"It is a grave loss to you Joseph, now Adnam is not entering your shipping and trading business. Adnam is a gentle and loving soul Joseph. Your blessing is that Adnam will be very close to the King. He will be able to watch over and safeguard your extensive interests in the metals and trading business, which will be a blessing if we have to flee from the Romans with the Disciples to Britain, and the Tin Island".

SAILING FOR SPAIN
JOSEPH IN CONVERSATIONS WITH JESUS

Standing on the stern of the ship, whilst Joseph was busy checking the tallies, Jesus stared out to the sea and the tin island disappearing into the horizon. Jesus was pondering the fact that life at the Druid Cor was such a life changing experience. Remembering as a small boy sitting on a rock in a Grove of trees staring up at the Druid teacher thinking how impossible it was to try to even imagine spending the next fifteen years at this place. It seemed an eternity.

His thoughts were broken as Joseph rested his firm hand on his shoulder. My son Adnam Josephus is in that horizon Jesus. He remains there, safe from the Roman filth. Part of both of us remains there in the horizon Jesus, but with you beside me I do not feel lonely and sad. I feel excited inside that after all these years, all my plans, all my hopes and wishes, everything is working out. At last we are starting our mission.

The road ahead will be painful and hard, but with my wealth we can take a message that will give our people a new hope. A hope that will lift them up from their hardship and despair. Jesus turned and looked at Joseph. "My first message to our people Joseph will be of my vision. That God is not the God of the Jews alone. God is the loving and forgiving Spirit of all mankind. I tell you this Joseph, rich or poor, high or low born, whatever race colour or creed. All men are equal in God's eyes. No man is above another. God is the God of all mankind. No one can put God in a box. No man can gain favour with God by paying money for a burnt offering. No man will gain favour with God making a great show of his religion before men. We must be wary of any group who say we are the way to God. Come with us. Excluding all others. These people are planning to gain power over a man and his money. Many will come with filth and fornication in God's name. The Priests will smile and welcome them and that will be the sign that the end is nigh. For those there will be a special place where they will be smitten and cursed".

"For all that I have learned Joseph, and all that you have seen. Our peoples are so very behind the peoples at our Ports of call". "Yes Jesus, I see enslavement, murder, rape and theft, all consistent with the attitudes of the occupying Romans and their evil ways. But this is why our mission is so important. The Romans are the cursed of God. There will be no eternal life for time and eternity for them. There is no hope for them. They will fall and disappear in time. We will go on to be born in another".

HOW EVOLUTION WORKS

It seems to me Jesus that over the period when Moses was leading our people from Egypt into the promised land, the peoples of this Tin Island were mining, smelting and casting the tools of great strength which they were shipping together with ingots to other lands. This enabled the people of Britain to farm their land, make cutters for taking the wool from their sheep; shipping pieces of metal to harness and control their horses and mules. Tools for every manner of living, including for the weaving of cloth. Weapons with which to defend themselves.

Do you see that this is the reason why the peoples of Britain are far more advanced in many ways than our own peoples and those of the Ports we visit. Britain is a land where the people do not have to struggle every day for their daily bread. They have the tools and crops and animals around them. They have surplus to their needs. They have store for winter, and food and goods to barter and sell. Animals of burden to carry 'goods' to barter and sell in exchange for luxury goods. Metal weapons with which to defend their families and villages.

These people will grow, advance and develop new things to their advantage. In the lands we visit where peoples toil all day for the days meagre bread. These nations will not advance and develop, or at least their advance will be very slow over time. Whereas those nations with all the advantages; tools, weapons, animals and carriages will enslave the slower, less developed peoples. This has happened in our own lands. We are enslaved to the Roman filth.

How is it Jesus that God gave his message to Moses to lead our people out from Egypt into the promised land using the ancient trade routes to the water holes enabling them to survive and grow in number. What the Jews did not have were the metals from which to make and cast weapons, tools, and harnesses for animals. It was obvious to the Jewish Elders that without these materials, the Jewish peoples would not make the advances necessary to keep our enemies at bay. In their wisdom our Elders sent a colony of Jews to Marseilles and the Tin Island of Britain to learn about these new materials, although our people did not have the wealth to buy their materials in quantities for our homeland. In Galilee we have only crops and fish. Judea has much less than we Galileans. Our nation will always be vulnerable to attack and takeover by others".

DISEMBARKING AT THE PORT OF MARSEILLES

Walking along the quayside Jesus felt a tightening in his throat when he became suddenly aware that his friend and companion for fifteen years, Adnam Josephus, was not walking beside him, but was back on the Isle of Avalon. Jesus stopped in his tracks, as he felt an overwhelming urge to flee back to the ship and return to Britain. After a short pause Jesus took a deep breath and felt his panic fade away as he reminded himself that he had a mission to fulfil that could not be avoided. Jesus, nevertheless felt empty and alone. A strange feeling he had not before experienced or felt. Everything around him was just a meaningless noise. Quite different to the happy Port he remembered.

JESUS HEALS A BLIND BOY

At that moment bright, almost blinding sunrays burst through the clouds. Jesus looked down. He felt tugging on his robe. There was a small boy, obviously blind, begging for alms. Jesus crouched down, holding the boy gently by the shoulders. "What is the greatest gift I can give you little man", asked Jesus. The boy replied, "If I could see everything around me from just one eye, I would be a slave to you for the rest of my life". Jesus looked into the boy's eyes. They were badly congested, in need of cleaning away the flies resting on his eyelids. Jesus took an ointment and a cloth from his robe, and proceeded to clean the boy's eyes with the ointment, after which Jesus discarded the cloth and rose slowly to his feet. A great scream issued from the boys mouth. "I CAN SEE. I CAN SEE. What miracle is this, I can see". Alarmed, traders from nearby stalls came running over to the boy.

"How is it you can see?" asked the stall holders. "The Master has cured my blindness. Now I must be his slave for life". "No, not so", replied Jesus. "I tell you this little man. Make this promise to Me. In all your lifetime you will do harm to no man, and that you will give to those that ask. Your promise will be My reward, and the reward of My God that has healed you". The crowd grew around Jesus as the boy told everyone he was cured of his blindness. Jesus slipped away half walking, half running to the ship. Jesus spoke out loudly to himself "If there was any doubt in My mind about returning to my Homeland, it is gone, for My God has spoken to me this day".

Jesus walked up the gangplank onto the deck, and stood leaning on the balustrade, looking out over the quayside. Jesus could see Joseph in the distance returning from Carcassonne. He was now surrounded by a number of traders. Joseph stopped at the foot of the gangplank and bid his leave of the traders. Joseph stepped off the plank, fixing ropes across so that none could board. Joseph stood beside Jesus. The traders shouted up from the quay. "Allow us to come aboard Joseph and talk to your healer. Let the healer stay with us on shore and share our hospitalities for a while". Joseph waved back and called "I am sorry, but we have to sail on the tide for we have a schedule that we must keep. Others in Rome are waiting delivery of their goods also".

Joseph looked across to Jesus. I heard about the healing of the boy who was blind Jesus. It is a wonderful thing you have done. I was going about God's business Joseph. The blind boy did not deserve to remain in his fate. This afternoon I missed Adnam Josephus. Me too Jesus, for he is my son, but our glory is to allow his will to be done, and not ours.

CONVERSATIONS WITH JESUS
SPIRITUAL AND PHYSICAL HEALING

My son Adnam told me Jesus, that you are the most sought after healer in the whole of the Druid Cor. Adnam said that many Druids claim you have performed many miracles of healing. That you healed a man whose eyes were so congested that his sight had left him, and when the man returned to the Cor, bringing with him gold coins you refused to accept the coins. Instead you instructed the man to give the coins to those less fortunate than himself as a token of his gratitude for his healing by the one God.

What secrets have you learned from the Druids Jesus, that have helped you achieve such success as a healer?"

"We were taught an extensive knowledge of ointments and herbal potions with which to treat many different ailments, Great Uncle Joseph. It is to my own astonishment that I remember every remedy for so many physical illnesses. Also those for treating the mind of man, including trance meditation, and the way of casting out devils. Even people harbouring an inner neurotic desire to remain an invalid can be cured through strong spiritual faith. The most stubborn infirmities can be cast out into animals".

"It is necessary for all successful healers to understand the fundamental make-up of a man. The Spirit of man is from God. The physical man is from the animal. Man shares his life with his animal nature. Some men more so than others. Spiritual disorders, whether conscious or below the conscious level result from Sin. The guilty feelings that come from Sin induce illness into the physical body. Sometimes the whole man is ill, requiring both spiritual and physical treatment.

If an illness persists, there have been occasions when I have made an amulet ring of silver, copper, or gold. Engraved flee, flee, and the name of the illness, followed by the words, "God has set me free". A combination of physical, mental and spiritual illness are not uncommon. It is therefore necessary for the healer to have sufficiently charged spiritual power to forge an invisible link between the spiritual and physical realms.

Strength of spirit can heal phobias, fears, lack of confidence, dizziness, fainting and much more. Strong spiritual suggestion should be accompanied by the application of herbal paste or the drinking of an appropriate infusion. There will be many maladies I can cure, and cripples I can heal, when we return to our own lands Joseph".

"That is important Jesus. On my many round trips from Joppa, along the trading centres to Britain; returning to my brother Joachim's house in Joppa four or five times every year I have seen the suffering of the sensitive of spirit. The elderly becoming ill from fear of the cruelty of the Roman soldiers. Other illnesses result from insufficient food when crops are poor or fail altogether. Stress and mental illnesses can result from being unable to make sacrifices at the Temple on feast days due to having no money".

"The healer must exert a powerful spiritual presence, Joseph, so that the patient can know without words the healer is a man of goodness and pure truth. This will forge the invisible, spiritual link. Quietness then engulfs the patient. Further suggestions linked to faith in the power of God and the Holy Spirit, are the substance of confidence and hope for the future. The healing that will take place is not a miracle, but the natural process of nature. It is the achievement of psychic motivation in the patient's subconscious mind that helps in the process of becoming well, because fear and despair are wiped away and the body can work its curative process.

Our Druid teachers taught us that healing of the physical body were best achieved by either the dispensing of herbal infusion, to be drunk as a medicine, or the application of herbal paste to affected parts of the body. Most herbs were grown in the Druid gardens or groves. We were taught to gather herbs by our own efforts. Then followed the processes of infusing by heating water, or grinding herbs into paste and mixing with oils.

Shortly after the treatments had been administered, effort was concentrated from our own physical powers to focus on healing the whole person".

CHOOSE FRIENDS CAREFULLY

Evil thought and wicked actions can trigger long term illness Joseph. Unfortunately thoughts in an evil mind can be transferred orally to the minds of others. What we learn from this is that we must choose carefully in life those people with whom we choose to associate, and those who we choose to be our friends. We must also guard against what we think, what we see, and what we may hear. No man should envy or admire an evil one for his time will be cloudy and short. They go down to the pit. No man can imagine the terrors they will face. Not for the evil spirit is time and eternity".

Spiritual Healing

We teach the patient that God's Spirit is the grace that entices man, but does not compel. Mans failure in his personal life often brings about illnesses, and problems effecting the workings of the body. However, until the man adjusts his life to God's way, spiritual healing cannot take place, whereas a life lived in God's way leads to a mentally balanced, healthier, happier, and longer life. Private prayer and devotion is a way to replenish spiritual energy, and raise mans spirit to a higher plane, where all things are possible. Where both physical and spiritual healing can take place as one.

Our ultimate goal is to become a Son of God, and gain Divine Power. To achieve this we must possess sufficient spiritual energy with which to develop deep spiritual insight. Learning how to achieve spiritual healing in others, is all part of the process.

I encourage families to fix an amulet in the entrance to their homes, with a quotation from the Scriptures of their favourite prophet so that evil will bypass their door.

At each Port of Call on our journey home, I will use my knowledge of herbs to heal those on the quayside at each stop".

"You are truly a great healer and teacher Jesus. By your own efforts you have become a Son of God. Miracles you will perform in God's name".

Be Still to Know God

Many people with whom I have spoken on my travels outside the Druid Cor, hold within themselves a deep longing to hear of things abnormal or extraordinary, such as the casting of runes for foretelling; the casting down of woods of the stars, and the heavens. Some even yearn to hear of conversations with ghostly spirits, of dead ancestors.

I have seen that some of this phenomena is self deception, unconscious falsification, or trance. Only Prophesy, a true treasure that fulfils the Prophets, is merit. I teach instead that it is better to be still and pray to know The Powers of the Universe, and step inside the knowledge of all things.

To find the truth of guidance in prayer, it is necessary to create a space, exercising patience, to allow the coming together in that space of Prayer and Holy Spirit. There shall be no evil thoughts, only that which is clean and wholesome and good, within that space. The space will expand over time to slowly fill the whole body, bringing about change and fulfilment as a new inner eye opens to witness the becoming of one with the Sons and Daughters of God. Then the path to eternal life opens ahead with sure stepping stones into a bright future.

It is necessary to work hard in fulfilling our earthly life by following what is honest and good. Only then will the longings and wishes in our prayers be fulfilled. It is within our own hands to make our prayers come good, by remembering that in matters of this earthly world, prayer and meditation are a wise support, but not a substitute for fact".

"For my part Jesus, I will use my wealth to help build more Meeting Houses in Galilee and Judea, to bring our new message of hope to our peoples. That God is a loving God. Our God is a forgiving God. That everyone, no matter what wealth, race, colour, or creed, everyone is equal in God's sight. No man is above another. No man can buy God's favours through sacrifice at the Jewish Temple in Jerusalem or by making a great show of his religion before men. This is the message your followers will take to all the peoples at each Port of Call on our journey to our Tin Island in Britain.

Words cannot express to you my Great Godson, Jesus, how proud I am in my heart at your success at the Druid Cor. My Son's appointment as High Priest to the King. And your decision to head the Missions in Judea and Galilee. I will not sleep this night for my heart is full of joy.

My Spirit tells me Jesus, that we are together embarking on a great journey that will be remembered through time and eternity, and that your dead father will know of your journey. Others will use your great knowledge and ability Jesus to gain power, authority, position and wealth for themselves. It is the way of man".

Sailing to Rome
Conversations with Jesus
Mysticism

Resting comfortably on deck after leaving Port, sailing away from the hustle and bustle noise of loading or offloading, is one of the enjoyable parts of any journey. Particularly when Joseph had achieved his objectives.

Sitting on deck with Jesus, Joseph asked Jesus to explain, what to Joseph has always been a puzzle to him. Enlighten me Jesus, what did the Druid High Priests teach you about Mysticism.

"Mysticism Joseph is not a man's opinion. Has nothing to do with the magic or the occult. Is not a confidence trick. Mysticism is an intuitive power dwelling below the threshold of consciousness. To raise mysticism into consciousness, it is necessary for all parts of the mind to work together as one. Mysticism can then be raised above the level of consciousness to a state of super consciousness, a level where the mind is able to know the unknowable. This results from the unfolding of consciousness of everyday world to reveal the reality of the existence of a higher super consciousness surrounding the everyday world.

Explained as an illuminated vision of the world; all its nature and its future. A mental state that is radically different to normal due to the splendour of its intensity. Also an awareness that the mind is not contained only within the confines of the brain.

There follows a growing awareness of the Divine. Lovable, infinitely capable, obtainable, alive, melting and fusing into awareness of God and Holy Spirit. Imageless, numbingly beautiful. Illuminating a new centre of self, of life, new destiny of self. All no less real than the everyday world. Plus the assurance that life really is eternal.

A Mystic is someone who through simple meditation or transcendental meditation is able to draw all parts of the mind to work together as one, to achieve the mentally altered state of super consciousness that permits emergence of the powerful transcendental self. Personal will and harmony draw close to the Mind of God, to become one with the family of the Sons of God and Daughters of God. Surpassing the plane of day to day reality, even unto supernatural reality. Leading to an awareness that God, as The Holy Spirit, is operating in the world day and night. That life itself is eternal. That the Holy Spirit is the Divine.

A mystic is someone who knows that the Holy Spirit can reside within a Priest in a church, or a devotee following a religion in India, or any man or woman who keeps God's Commandments. They may be sitting in prayer or meditation in a room in their home or anywhere, in any place in the world.

A mystic is someone who knows that the Holy Spirit will flee far from anyone living in sin or fornication of any kind, including any religio living in sin and fornication.

A mystic is aware that anyone entering religion for the purpose of gaining personal adoration, respect, or prestige, substituting their personal vanity in the stead of God, and the Holy Spirit before men, is evil.

A mystic becomes aware that the Holy Spirit is the most powerful force permeating the planet without contravening the natural laws of nature or the laws of the universe.

A mystic is someone who knows that any establishment or group that claims to own or control access to God and the Holy Spirit to the exclusion of every other group may be a force for evil.

After many years of training and practice Joseph, I am able to slip into meditation at any level when I need to refresh my faith by feeling very close to the Divine. But it is not a means of escapism or overcoming reality. One always returns to now, but feeling refreshed, alive and confident in one's own ability to overcome; be a beacon to others. Meditation and prayer cost nothing but they are a safe port in a storm to those who are lost and unhappy or in despair".

SAILING FOR ATHENS
CONVERSATION WITH JESUS

As you are aware Jesus, the Athenians have wealth and independence because they have much silver from their own resources. It will be useful to barter for silver goblets and plates, which are cheaper than in any other Port. We will take what we achieve in barter onto Judea. I will tempt traders into bartering silver in exchange for luxury materials to use in the making of clothing. However, our anchor will be overnight only. We must sail tomorrow to keep to my schedule".

Anchored under the stars, with no swell and a steady breeze, and only the creaking of the ships timbers, Joseph and Jesus were laying completely relaxed seated in two coils of rope taking turns in recognising star patterns, when Joseph asked Jesus. What did your Druid teachers reveal about the beliefs of those living in Britain outside the Druid religion.

CELTIC BELIEFS

Jesus answered "The tribes believed that there is a domain below ground peopled with Gods and dead tribal ancestors. A supernatural world where their Gods can determine tribal fate relating to crops, animals and the fate of the individual. Dead relatives were buried in a tribal vault. A strict ceremony was followed to erect a stone in memory of the dead. If this process were not followed in detail, it was thought that crops could fail through lack of rain, and tribal members would die of a fever. Follow the ceremony in detail, and crops will flourish. Animals will multiply successfully and yield plenty of milk. The Gods would keep animals free from disease.

Their leaders taught that it was also necessary to keep the Gods in the underground kingdoms happy with gifts, but these gifts had to be new and unused. Gangways walked over flooded areas from where gifts such as new metal tools, or handles, were cast into the water during either the time of the New or Full Moon and all would be well. They named the leading God Janus, who also had a brother".

THE FIRST INDUSTRIAL REVOLUTION

Beyond the Mendip Hills there was a great open pit where the green copper ore was dug. Even children dug into the sides of the pit to free the ore from the soil.

Copper would be brought to the Jews Houses, where smelters would mix copper and tin to make bronze from which they cast tools for all manner of uses. Tools that would be far stronger and more enduring than antlers. Also preferred to tools made from flint. Dug out boats would travel round the coast to meet up with ships from the European trade routes to barter and trade the new strong tools. However, only the Jews Houses were the masters of casting bronze and extracting silver from the lead in the Mendip Hills.

The Druid Priest called this a great revolution. Such was the joy of seeing ore transformed into shining tin or silver, and the casting into tools. Everyone would sing Joseph Is a Tin Man, in praise of Jews and to ensure good luck whilst the process was taking place.

Only the Romans would view these techniques as a gift for making weapons to be used for death, destruction and slavery.

SILVER WATER CURES DISEASE

"As you know Joseph, we were taught at the Druid Cor to leave drinking water overnight in our silver goblets to rid water of disease. It was also necessary to treat all water to be used in infusions in the same way. Silver water was one of our most popular cures, because it could heal many diseases. The King drank silver water every day to keep himself in good health".

A wine chalice said to have been used at the Last Supper, in the possession of the Rayner Family. Chalices used were carved from marble on a pole style lathe, soaked in honey then baked to bring out the fine radiant colours in the marble. Some chalices were made using marble cups mounted on a silver base. Imported to Cornwall by Joseph of Arimathea. There is evidence from fragments in historic texts that the Grail Chalices brought to England by St. Joseph were of beaten silver.

JESUS ARRIVES IN ISRAEL

Arriving at the Port of Joppa, Israel, after an absence of fifteen years, Jesus breathed deeply to take in and taste the warm air he knew so well as a child. Jesus commented to Joseph that the temperature in Joppa was so very different to that to which he had become accustomed at the Druid Cor. Air, fresh and stimulating from the lands to the North of Britain, carrying recognisable fragrances from each changing season.

"I have to remember Joseph the teachings of my Druid teachers, not to visit or dwell on the past. The past must be dealt with in order to enable us to move on into the future, with all our wounds healed, remembering only useful knowledge gathered during the past".

Joseph called to Jesus, "The crew have a full load to transfer from the ship to the store this night. The crew will work late and sleep in the store where they will feel secure and happy surrounded by an atmosphere of plenty. Some goods will remain on board for transport up to Capernaum and Tyre. You and I Jesus will travel on with my pack mules and burden bearers to my brother Joachim's house in Arimathea".

"Your Grandparents Joachim and his wife Ann will be thrilled and surprised at your presence. They will not recognise you now you have grown to manhood and filled out with your strength. They can never know or understand what great knowledge and powers you have accumulated over the years at the Druid Cor. My older brother Joachim will scold me for not visiting home on my last hurried visit to Joppa. He may also call me to account for not going up to the Temple to greet the Temple Priests; where both my name and Nicodemus have apparently moved up the list of seniority. A list jealously guarded and squabbled over by the Temple Priests. Let it be so, but I am confident in my own mind that we know so much more about the truth of God and God's ways than all the Temple Priests in their great wheel of hubris. I must remember to keep my conversations guarded Jesus, less I be excluded from the Sanhedrin".

Jesus replied, "The biggest problem we have to overcome in this land Great Uncle Joseph is persuading Jewish Priests that all men are equal in the eyes of God. No one can buy God's favours with the sprinkling of blood from animal sacrifice. God requires all mankind to transcend unevolved primitive ideas and very ancient tribal customs and traditions. Only then will man understand that God is the all powerful Holy Spirit that permeates all men who keep God's Commandments.

49

I fear Joseph that the Temple Priests with their animal sacrifices, sprinkling of blood and burnt offerings and other rituals performed in their grand robes, is a barrier to their crossing the spiritual bridge from Temple Judaism to the real God and the true Holy Spirit".

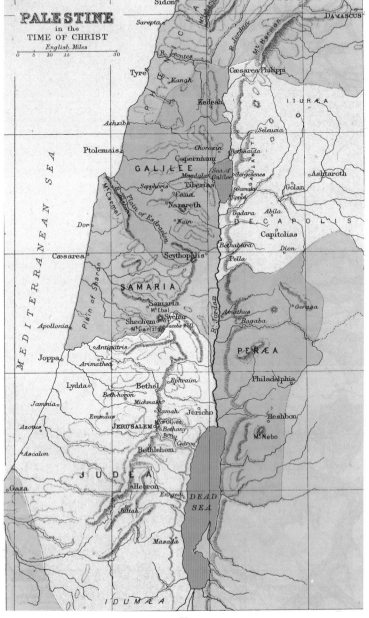

First Stop Arimathea

Jesus, Joseph, and their burden bearers arrived at Joseph's home in Arimathea in darkness. Joseph banged on the stout wooden door at the top of a flight of cobbled steps. No response, but heads started to pop out from windows lit by oil lamps. Suddenly there were great shouts of joy as Joseph's brother Joachim appeared at the open door with a large hand held oil lamp. Ann, his wife, stood beside him weeping tears of joy.

"Bring your burden bearers with their loads into the stables where they may sleep this night on the heated pedestal", Joachim called down the steps. "I will prepare food and juice of freshly pressed grapes that everyone may eat and drink their fill. They will sleep soundly on a heated platform with a full stomach on dry land this night". Joachim and Ann both eyed the fine strong upright figure of a handsome man standing erect in silence, behind Joseph.

Both asked in their minds, could this be our Grandson Jesus, so tall and so fine, who had been studying in Britain on the Isle of tin these many years, and has performed many miracles? They both fell silent as tears of joy whelmed up in their eyes. They both hoped and prayed that this fine stranger whose power emanated from his very presence was their Grandson they had heard so much about on Joseph's many return journeys home from Britain.

Jesus Meets Joachim and Ann

Ann could stand the suspense no longer. "Are you Jesus? Can you be Jesus our Grandson?" Joseph stepped forward. "Ann, God has blessed you both this day", replied Joseph. "This is your Grandson Jesus about whom I told you so much". Ann fell on her knees before Jesus, grabbing his ankles and crying uncontrollably, for reasons neither Joachim nor Joseph could understand. Joachim helped Ann slowly and gently to her feet. "Come Ann, this is no occasion for sorrow and tears. Let us eat and drink together with our guests who have come on such a long and arduous journey to be with us this night".

Laying on their wool mattresses after the celebration Jesus called over to Joseph. "I am yearning Joseph for the views from my home in Nazareth. The view across the valleys to Mt. Carmel. As far as the Jordan Valleys and hill of Gilead. On a clear day I could see the snow covered Mt. Hermon. Below were the olive groves and vineyards. It was an easy journey downhill to the road between Caesarea on the coast, the headquarters of the Roman Legions and only three hours walk to the lake".

As dawn broke Ann greeted Jesus and Joseph with a silver chalice each of goats milk, bread, and goats cheese on a large silver salver. Both men rose and went to the table, Ann seated herself in front of Jesus. Ann gazed intensely at Jesus as he was eating. "I remember Jesus that I was passed the age of conceiving a child, when scrying with his crystal, a Priest from the East who was our guest overnight, announced that I was to give birth to your mother Mary. You are truly a miracle child from a miracle mother. Joseph has told us about your achievements in Britain, Jesus, and the queues of people waiting at the Cor to be healed. We are also very proud that our grandson, Adnam Josephus, has been appointed Arch Druid to King Arviragus. We shall all clearly miss Adnam, but it is for his will to be done not ours".

"Is it possible Jesus that you have returned to save us from the beastial Romans. It is not safe for us to venture out into the market square without Roman soldiers helping themselves to the fruits of our purchases. Even young children, both boys and girls are not safe from molestation by the Roman filth. Please comfort me Jesus, tell me you have come to save us from the Romans". "I have come to save, but not in a way you will yet understand", replied Jesus.

New Life in the Twinkling of an Eye

Please do not worry so much about your lives Joachim and Ann. When your time is come, you will pass over in the twinkling of an eye to a new life you have earned by the manner in which you have lead your lives here in Jerusalem. You will not even be aware of your passing, and in the life in which you will arrive, you will have no memory of the pain you have endured witnessing the Romans flourish and prosper in spite of their evil ways", said Jesus.

Still influenced by the routine of the Druids at the Druid Cor, Jesus and Joseph rose early to make their way through the sleepy villages with their burden bearers and pack mules. Approaching the City Gates Jesus remarked to Joseph about the large number of Roman soldiers all around. "Do not draw the attention of the Roman soldiers, Jesus. The soldiers will not trouble us because we are on official business". Well dressed and obviously senior Roman figures nodded acknowledgement of Joseph's greetings.

As they walked into the Temple precincts. Jesus called to Joseph. "Why are there tables and money changers in this sacred place. How can this be Joseph?" "Be calm Jesus, much has changed in the past fifteen years since you were here as a boy".

"All the traders at these tables are paying a levy to the Temple. Some even work for the Temple Priests, and share in the profits to be made, which can be very substantial on feast days".

"Come over Jesus. Allow me to introduce you to the Temple Priests". Close by were a group of Priests, clearly deep in discussion about their profits and gains. Full of jollity, they did not notice either Joseph or Jesus watching their every move.

ANGER OF JESUS

Jesus was angry, appealing to Joseph that these Priests, the stewards of God's Temple have allowed the Temple to become a whore, a den of thieves. "I tell you Joseph, when millennium have passed, God has already put in place those who will tear down this Temple, not leaving one stone upon another. I tell you Joseph when millenniums have passed there will arise in Rome another great whore such as this Temple, with Priests wearing expensive gowns, claiming to be God's sons on earth. Outside their precincts parentless children will starve".

ROME WILL DISAPPEAR

Such will be God's wrath of these vile actions committed in His name by them. The Earth will wrent open and that Temple will be swallowed, and there will be much wailing as we have not yet heard". Let us return to my home early Joseph instructed Jesus, for tomorrow we must travel early to Joppa to ready the ship for our sail to Capernaum.

"You must be excited Jesus, tomorrow we travel to your home in Nazareth to greet your mother Mary and your brothers and sisters. They will be eagerly awaiting their presents and gifts. While we sojourn at your home the burden bearers can deliver the new nets we have brought for my fishermen. They can then pay for some pack mules and travel to Mary Magdalene to collect the salted fish and one piece garments Mary has been storing at her home. The burden bearers may then hand over the last of the orders to Mary's ferry to deliver to the villages around the lake and collect payment".

Jesus told Joseph that he was eager to meet with Mary Magdalene to hear the latest news from the Meeting Houses around the Galilee. "We must place Mary Magdalene in charge of the women of the Meeting Houses round the Galilee. We must also arrange for the construction of a Meeting House for Mary in Magdala".

"I have never ceased to amaze at the wondrous ability of my father Joseph. All our close families are fellahs the farmers; my father Joseph was as you know, the best builder in the district. Capable of building and making in wood and stone: to raise even the largest dwellings in a short space of time. Always he built stone steps to the roof so no one would be caught by fire".

"I long for the one piece cloaks Jesus; in each colour, red, blue, and purple, for which the women of Galilee are famous. There is not a cloak more comfortable to wear sleeping outside under the stars or when travelling", said Joseph.

"Why was the Great Temple built in Judea Joseph? When I hear a wind instrument, I picture the Sea of Galilee shaped like a harp and surrounded by fertile plains; valleys with crops growing on terraces. Olive groves, vineyards, and pasture for the animals. Surely Joseph the land of Adam. Galilee is always so busy, criss-crossed as it is with caravans of burden. Camels, laden donkeys and pack mules, carrying barrels of salted fish, dried fruits, corn, olive oil, unfermented wine, wool dyed or plain in colour. Glass, silver chalices, and all manner of spices and incense.

By comparison Judea is a road to nowhere. Comprising mountainous deserts, narrow rain starved valleys with poor quality cracked and dry soil. If it were not for the olive and grape orchards, the people would face great hardship. Most trade routes also pass by Judea along the coastal routes. The roads to the Temple pass along nothing more than dry dusty roads through the farms and villages where people are really struggling to have sufficient food to eat. Joseph told Jesus that the people are kept poor by Roman Taxes. Every day they have to worry about their daily bread.

"The Temple Vaults are busting with gold, silver, and preserved foods, whilst these people have nothing. These people long for a Messiah to come and save them from the Romans and the double taxation on what little they earn, Jesus".

After the experience of seeing for himself that the Temple in Jerusalem had been turned into a place of grandeur and profit centre, while the people of the villages all around were sometimes close to starvation, Jesus felt a relief boarding the ship to sail to the Port of Tyre, where he could put the memory behind him, at least for a while, of unhappy starving people.

Laying on deck under the stars, Jesus could not sleep for the tension of the excitement he felt inside; seeing his mother after so many years. How his three brothers and two sisters will have grown into adulthood. The passing of his father. Jesus was not sad. His father appeared on the ship and said his goodbye. Jesus knew his father was going on to a wonderful life he had earned by his fruitful life and love of God. His father would have no memory of his past life, but he was going on to a lifetime of joy and happiness that had been hard earned.

Jesus called out to Joseph "we must also ask Mary to arrange to gather together her many followers to hear My address. I will appoint Mary as my first Disciple before the crowd. Then I will address the crowd and tell them of God's plan. However, before that address I will need to recruit Disciples". Joseph replied in an authoritative voice. "Do not be anxious Jesus. I own the fishing fleet on the Galilee, as you are aware. I will instruct my men that those amongst them who choose to go with you on your mission, may do so on full pay, for as long as it takes to expand the Meeting Houses from the Galilee to Judea. God has provided for all your needs".

Joseph could hear Jesus continue in his restlessness twisting and turning. Joseph called across "If you are awake Jesus tell me what the Druids taught you of our one God".

THERE IS A GOD

God expresses presence as a formless energy, known to us as the Holy Spirit. Forever unfolding by coming into existence for some. Always absent from existence for others. Both in and out of existence for the great many.

For those aware of mortality and judgement, the Holy Spirit comes into consciousness, giving life meaning, shape, guidance and healing; spiritual vision of eternity. The vision that resolves all the future into the most advantageous future for the faithful, through portals not thought to exist. Holy Spirit. Its spiritual meaning does not come into existence for the many sinners. For them, only repentance will open the portals to eternal life.

Jesus and Joseph Head for the Galilee

As Jesus and Joseph left the Home of Jesus and headed for the Galilee, Jesus waved frantically to his mother and brothers and sisters until they were out of sight. Both men walked and climbed in silence in anticipation of who might be waiting to greet them on their arrival. Joseph had related to Jesus so many good reports about Mary Magdalene, that Jesus was anxious to meet Mary for he barely remembered Mary from his childhood. Jesus and Joseph stopped in their tracks as they rounded a bend in the road and the water of the Galilee came into view. Jesus was surprised to see a crowd of Galileans at the bottom of the footpath. Jesus looked over to Joseph but Joseph said nothing and smiled. As both men neared the gathering, a roar went up accompanied by much clapping and jollity.

A woman stepped forward, peering out from a veil that covered her head. "Welcome home Jesus. Welcome to the Galilee". More clapping ensued. "We have heard so many exciting tales of your miracles of healing on the Tin Island in Britain. Many in the crowd have been waiting since first light. Some have come carrying the sick for you to heal their infirmities and pain".

Jesus Greets Mary Magdalene

I am Mary Magdalene. I lead the women of the Meeting Houses on the Galilee. My family are part owners and run the ferry and conduct your Godfather Joseph's business in these parts. I have been visiting your Mother Mary with women from the Meeting Houses to comfort and help her after the death of your father. Such a wonderful man, and a great loss to these parts. We, all of us, have been eagerly awaiting your return for Joseph told us the time was near. Joseph has been our Storyteller on each return trip. So wonderful and masterful were his tales of the miracles and wonders you have performed on the Tin Islands. The crowds have grown to the extent that many at the back of the crowd could barely hear Joseph's voice".

Jesus became aware in his mind that Joseph had arranged this welcoming party. Jesus also realised that his family had followed them to the Galilee at a distance not to spoil Joseph's surprise. Mary his mother and his sisters came up behind Jesus and gave him a hug. Mary called out, "This is my Son of whom I am well pleased, but no mother should love one of her children above another". Joseph called over to Mary Magdalene, "Allow me to first run over the business to the gathering, so that we may hear from Jesus, and then commence our celebrations".

PLEASE MARRY MARY MAGDALENE

Mary went up to Jesus. Jesus could see that his Mother had tears of joy on her face. He gently placed his hands over hers. She looked up into his eyes. "Will you marry Mary Magdalene My Son. Please marry Mary, for she is your promised, your betrothed. Everyone living in Nazareth and Galilee, in the hills around would come to celebrate such a magnificent occasion. Please hear my words Jesus. Your father, my husband is gone. I need you and Mary here with Me to carry on our seed".

"I hear and understand your words my Mother, and I love you with all my heart, but Mary and I are married to God. There is no greater destiny upon this earth than being married to God. Our destiny is far greater and more important than becoming man and wife in human kind. We have our mission. A mission that will change the destiny of mankind forever. Mary and I are already married in our Souls". "I do not know your words Jesus. I do not understand what you say. Are you but a stranger to Me after so many years at the Druid Cor?"

"Do not cry Mother. Hear My promise. You will understand. You will see Me in greater glory than marriage. You will become changed by this Glory that is coming to you. You cannot see at this time what greatness awaits you. There is a love that transcends all understanding. Greater than the affairs of man. Greater than a mother for her child. The same is My love for God, the Holy Spirit".

"Your faith will save your Soul Jesus, but it will not save you from a Roman Spear". "Our Soul is not our body Mother. This is part of the great mystery I have to unfold with Mary and our Disciples to our people. They must cast off the old and bring in the new. They must give up the thinking of the ages past, and open their Souls to the light. Any evil Roman can kill our body, but they cannot kill our Soul because it is not in our body, or within the physical world. Our Souls will pass on to Time and Eternity".

"I tell you from My heart My Mother. You will feel the Rapture when it comes. You will see Me in Gods Glory. I promise that the Rapture is coming to you My Mother. You will feel the love that is greater than love in humankind".

Joseph stood on the tallest rock. "I have brought to you from the Tin Island new nets to replace the old shabakeh. I am aware that some may not wish to place their trust in a new net. I urge you to use existing nets and the new nets on either side of your vessel. When you have trawled using both nets, you will soon become aware of the superiority of the new nets. However, I will leave the matter to your own judgement. My next request is to start using the barrels I have brought from the Tin Island to store your salted fish, because the fish will store for longer than in the flat sacks".

JOSEPH APPOINTS DISCIPLES

Please listen carefully to my new plan. Those fishermen amongst you who are from the Meeting Houses and who would like a new life supporting the Missions of Jesus to expand our Meeting Houses, may leave your boats to travel with Jesus, first around the Galilee and then down to Judea. You may recruit brothers or relatives to replace yourselves on your boats. We will support both yourselves and wives who may care to travel with you to cook and sew to support the group. We will provide for everything. All you need to concern yourselves with is the task of doing God's work. Jesus will now address you to explain the plans for a most exciting future for all".

JESUS ADDRESSES THE GALILEANS

Fishermen, brothers and sisters of Galilee. I bring only good news. There is a place in God's Kingdom for everyone, because our one God is a loving God. Our God loves everyone equally, whether rich or poor, high born or low born, whatever race, colour or creed. Everyone is equal in God's sight. No one man is above another. Our God is a forgiving God to those who fall on their knees in prayer and repent their sins and ask God's forgiveness. Those who keep God's Commandments will be surrounded by the Holy Spirit. Those who keep God's Commandments will never die, their spirit shall go on to Eternal Life. In the twinkling of an eye shall they leave their body and pass on to their new life with no recall of the past. This is the good news we shall take to the Meeting Houses on the Galilee. This is the good news we must spread throughout the land. So let us all rejoice and be glad. Let those who choose to follow me be aware that you will leave your nets and become fishers of men. All the Mothers of the Galilee will be your mother. All the women of the Galilee will be your sisters. We will spread this good news throughout the Galilee. Many will come to us. Many will not understand and go on their way. Those who remain will swell our numbers to seventy, when we will go down to Jerusalem where my brother James will build our church in that Holy place that has become a whore and a den of thieves".

When Jesus saw those scribes recording his words in their Greek he called out to them. "You scribes must learn God's words in your heart. You must keep God's words in your mind to govern your actions and your decisions every minute of every day".

"We must show our followers kinship, love, understanding and communion. In the Temple in Jerusalem the High Priests dress in their grand robes, performing ceremony and ritual, believing that a show of grandeur before men will bring them closer to God. In very truth God and the Holy Spirit do not see their grandeur and hear their great performance. God has already put in place those who will destroy the Temple in Jerusalem. There will not be one stone left standing upon another. I tell you this, God is looking for all of us to come together, and enjoying his love, the love of God, by keeping His commandments. Repenting and asking forgiveness for our sins. Sitting in prayer every day in the quiet of our room and place, being aware that the Holy Spirit is with us every minute of every day. Not fearing death because eternal life will be our reward. Feel clean, wholesome and good in body mind and spirit, and your days will be sunny in this land".

"In a millennium, a great whore will grow up in the filth of Rome, who will dress in grand robes with great ritual. Men who will cause murder, death, and suffering in God's name. God's greatest damnation will be for all those who cause death in God's name. No man can imagine the suffering and pain that will be mete out to these evil doers. Their suffering and pain will last for time and eternity. For is it not God's greatest Commandment "Thou shalt not kill". Is this not God's word from the time of Moses, "Thou shalt not kill". Anyone who kills in the name of God, or sends others to murder in the name of God, their's shall be the greatest of all eternal damnations always.

MARY MAGDALENE APPOINTED A DISCIPLE

Now it is time to announce that Mary Magdalene is appointed my First Disciple before God. Mary will be in charge of the women of the Galilee. There is nothing hidden that shall not be shouted from the highest roof top. I shall address Mary before all of you that you shall be God's witness. Stand before this rock on which I stand Mary that we make our oath before all our brothers and sisters".

"We must remain pure Mary so that our eyes remain singular looking only to God". Mary replied "I will accept your invitation to be your Disciple. I will remain pure Jesus, because I am now married to God". With that the couple embraced in front of the crowd and kissed on the mouth to seal the revelations that came out from their mouths as was the tradition of the day.

All who were watching were overcome with joy. Men and women were crying great tears while dancing, clapping and singing at the same time. Joseph was crying profusely when he stepped forward and laid his hands gently upon their heads. Joseph looked to Heaven. He cried out, "My God, My Daughter of God, My God, My Son of God".

JOSEPH ADDRESSES THE GALILEANS

Joseph stepped up onto a rock. The crowd fell silent. Joseph spoke out, "Do not stop your rejoicing, our joy has only just begun. But remember this day. For many of you this is the first day of a long exciting and fearful journey ahead. This day our journey has truly begun". Joseph slipped down from the rock amid much clapping and cheeping, rising from a crowd full of merriment and fun. Joseph wandered off with his right arm around the waist of Jesus and his left arm around the waist of Mary. "Today we have forged a new Meaning and new Revelation before our God. Revelations that will last for Time and Eternity within a story that will be told through time and eternity. You Jesus will remain pure of body and mind like all those who follow you to become the Sons of God. You Mary will remain pure of body and mind, Married only to God. All those who will follow you will become Married to God. Great is this day. Let us rejoice and be glad in it. I love you both, more than any words can convey. There is nothing more worthwhile that has grown up from a seed. Today, we have planted the seeds of Eternal Life. A life that lasts for time and eternity. Many shall be called, but only few will understand this calling and remain to be chosen".

SECRETS OF THE HOLY SPIRIT

Those who keep the Commandments of Moses and do harm to no one will experience mysterious happenings. The Holy Spirit does not send scribes to write letters, but will speak to you through others. Be wary therefore who you choose to be your friends. Always take your rest in peace, that the Holy Spirit may come to you in your dreams. The Holy Spirit will give you a sense of bad people. The Holy Spirit will put those in place who will warn and protect you. The Holy Spirit will put in place those who will help you achieve your dreams.

ESCAPE TO MARSEILLES AND AVALON

Any event at the Temple in Jerusalem was very big business. The main thrust of this business was the supply and sale of animals for sacrifice; whose blood would be sprinkled over the Temple Altar. Sacrifices ranged from a large ram to a small caged bird.

The choice of which depended upon the wealth of the Jewish buyer, and how much money they were prepared to spend to buy God's favour. All believing indirectly that God's favours are for sale. (Animal sacrifice and sprinkling of blood had been practiced around Africa for thousands of years).
As tradition, hundreds of doves were supplied from the hills of Magdala.

The Members of the Sanhedrin the Jewish ruling body of the Temple, controlled most of the business being conducted in and around the Temple precincts. Additionally, they controlled and supplied the Money Changers and those selling gold and silver. No money changed hands anywhere near the Temple without senior Members of the Sanhedrin receiving their cut.

Jesus, James and their Disciples preached against animal sacrifice, and against the Temple becoming a bustling market place. The Jewish Leaders at the temple were incensed at the Christian doctrine. No doubt their main concern was the fear that the teachings of the Jewish Christians would affect their income and Temple business.

CAPERNAUM

Joseph's ship anchored at sea off Capernaum, having completed a four month round trip to Britain. As soon as the ship anchored a hooded man rowed out and clambered on board looking for Joseph. Removing his headwear, the man, one of Joseph's fishermen from the Galilee, blurted out in an excited manner that when he was visiting a relative in Caesarea, he heard that an order had been received from Rome to arrest and question (the Romans' name for torture) all the known Christians in the Galilee. The order placed a price on the head of their leader, Mary Magdalene.

Lazarus and Phillip had sailed up from Joppa with Joseph. Both men were hauling up corn, olives, olive oil, wine, frankincense and woven matting. Joseph called down to Lazarus and Phillip, "I want you to leave now for the Galilee. Sail round the lake and warn all the Meeting Houses of the danger. Locate Mary Magdalene. Explain what has happened and bring her and Martha to the ship at nightfall, with as many others who want to leave".

DISCIPLES FLEE TO MARSEILLES AND BRITAIN

Mary Magdalene, Martha, Lazarus and Phillip and the Disciples who ran the Meeting Houses around the Galilee were rowed out from shore and boarded the ship just after first light. Joseph gave the order to cast off immediately, while the Romans were still sleeping. Joseph informed everyone that they would be sailing direct to Marseilles to avoid being overtaken by a fast Roman Galley.

JOSEPH ADDRESSES THE DISCIPLES

With everyone settled on deck enjoying the early morning sunshine, and not a ship in sight, Joseph took the opportunity to explain why Jesus had been arrested. Temple spies reported that at their open air meetings Jesus and his Disciples preached against animal sacrifice, and Money Changers turning the Temple and its precincts into a large bustling market and a den of thieves.

"The Disciples and Jesus were warned by followers that the Temple Priests were hatching a plan to persuade the Roman Governor, that Jesus and His followers were planning to overthrow Roman rule in Judea, and that Jesus and his followers were terrorists who must be tracked down and executed. Also that the Galilee, the area in which the Christians were gathering in strength must not remain a safe haven for these terrorists. I went with Mary, his mother and begged Jesus not to make the journey into Jerusalem on that fateful day. Jesus said he was going to the sacrifice but not in a way that would be understood by the Romans. We pleaded and cried but nothing we said would change his mind".

"Our life task is not to allow the death of Jesus to be in vain. Our mission will continue. I will organise everything from my new home on Britain's Tin Island, under the protection of the King and his army, and with the help of my son. I have the two goblets on which the 'Ritual of Eternal Life' is engraved. Each Disciple has the ritual engraved on his heart, and on his amulet. My traders at every port will provide each Disciple with everything they need. Every Disciple must travel on my ship to the Tin Island to visit the Meeting House I shall build dedicated to my Great Godson Jesus. Each supper we share together on our journey in this ship, we will pass the goblets used at the supper in Jerusalem before the arrest of Jesus. Each supper we will say a prayer to my Godson".

"Each night after supper we will enjoy the 'Ritual of Eternal Life'. We are the keepers of the secret of Eternal Life. A precious secret passed on to us by dear Jesus. Many will look for this secret, but only a few will find".

Mary, Martha and Phillip Reach Narbonne

Approaching Marseilles and to avoid the attention of any Roman galley, Joseph ordered the Captain to anchor downstream from the main port and opposite the beaches where the passengers would be landing. It would be too dangerous for Mary Magdalene to be seen near the main Port where Roman spies would be eager to claim their reward.

Luck was with them. There was a steady onshore breeze. The plan was for Phillip to take Mary and Martha ashore in the ship's tender, using a small sail, lashed as a fishing boat because a small fishing boat driving up onto a beach using the onshore wind should not attract any attention or interest. When all were aboard the tender, Joseph looked down on the small vessel with no oars, and a small sail looking like a bird's wing. Joseph knew from experience that the small vessel would be sufficient to carry the party to shore and onto the beach close to Narbonne from where they could walk to their friends and relatives at Carcassonne. There they would be safe amongst their neighbours, none of whom had any love for the Roman filth.

Joseph Sets Sail for Glastonbury

Preparing to cast off, Joseph called down to the tender, "Our God will protect you. My Captain will call upon you, and deliver supplies on his next trip". The tender cast off, swinging swiftly with the wind and headed for the shoreline. Joseph felt confident that all was well, and ordered the Captain to make sail for Britain's Glastonbury, where they would all be safe under the protection of the King and the King's substantial army. Joseph was so excited. He would be seeing his son Adnam Josephus. Not as a boy, but as a High Priest to the King. As Joseph reached his cabin he found he was still holding the two silver goblets he had brought with him from Capernaum. The goblet used to pass wine at the supper. The goblet used to prepare the body of Jesus both he and Nicodemus had taken down from the cross. Joseph sat on his bunk and cried uncontrollably. Joseph cried and cried and cried until his face soaked in tears. This crying gave way to sobbing. How am I going to tell Adnam? How am I going to tell Adnam? How am I going to tell Adnam that I did not prevent Jesus going to his death?

Still grasping the goblets and still fully clothed Joseph fell into a merciful sleep. Joseph woke up when the ship lurched. Placing the silver goblets inside his cloak Joseph called out in a loud voice. "I vow to you my God, I will not tire or rest until the Disciples of Jesus have finished their mission".

The Healing Of Sorrow

Joseph stretched out and waited.
Safely concealed in his robe
Within a shrine of silver and gold
The Holiest of Relics.

The sky shone with stars
The ground soft and sweet,
Horns sounding, Voices singing.
Joseph knew this was the time
The time of his healing, The time of truth.
The passage to Eternal Life.

Incense swept over him
As he was gently carried overhead
To the Sacred Grove.
The Place of Enchantment.

The mystics of the Lake followed in silence
Bearing fruits and berries.
Their lanterns glowing like the stars themselves.

Joseph drank the sacred cup
And floated to the secret world.

First came the golden glow of the Skull.
The Cave was filled with its beauty.
Here Merlin held the Red Crystal.
Here Arthur with his Sword and Shield, Guinevere by his side.
The Knights splendid in their Armour.
And then the Holy Abbey itself.

As he greeted them
Disciples shone from every corner
Leading him, showing him the path.
And then the Light. The Light of Jesus.

Joseph slept for two days.

Joseph lay on a bed of sweet healing herbs, Adnam by his side.
Come Father you have seen the truth
We must build this Church.
We must leave our hearts in this place.
Adnam my Son, I am ready,
I have been cured of Sorrow.

"Comfort yourself Joseph with the thoughts that whilst the Romans think they have completely silenced our missions, they are not aware that we have bigger fish to catch, and because mariners have wings to fly across the seas, everything is possible. In the meantime, James the brother of Jesus, will carry on our mission in Judea in and around Jerusalem".

Joseph rose slowly to his feet, placing his arm around the shoulder of Lazarus. "In Avalon Lazarus, we will all be safe. We will enjoy the protection and hospitality of King Aravagus, and his family. You cannot imagine Lazarus how much you have to see in Avalon and around that is new to your eyes. A world so different to Bethany and Judea, that you will be lost for words for many a day. You will delight in so many Jews houses producing tin and other metals where traders are queuing at their doors to buy the fruits of their labours. When we arrive Lazarus, you will eat and rest and enjoy yourself. This is my promise to you my dearest friend and supporter of my Godson".

FIRST CHURCH OUTSIDE JERUSALEM A.D.38

When you have rested Lazarus, I will explain my plan to build quickly the first Meeting House outside Jerusalem at Avalon. There we will worship and make plans to carry on our work. Disciples will reach out from all the Ports to which our ships travel from Avalon to Joppa. Our base will be here, but through our Disciples and brothers in God we will reach out from our sailing ships to many peoples in many lands. I have with me Lazarus the two silver chalices we passed around the table at our last supper in Jerusalem. When we meet, the Holy Spirit will be in Him and He will be in us.

I am going to my Garden of Eden Lazarus, to see my son and find solace for my heavy heart. What we have to remember Lazarus above all things is that this is the time for a new beginning. A time when Disciples can spread the Good News at every Port of call. I know Lazarus that I disagreed with Jesus at the manner in which He offered himself up to the slaughter in Jerusalem, but it was for his will to be done, and not my will to be done. We can be with Jesus again in Spirit when we offer the chalices round the table at supper on ship and in our new Meeting House at Glastonbury. Come Lazarus, We are both tired. So much has happened in the past days. Let us take our rest in prayer and sleep for tomorrow is a new beginning. Tomorrow we will be born again. When I have finished God's work, and on the day of my death, all of the chalices of the Holy Grail will be buried with me on my tin isle in my beloved Avalon. The other I shall commit to the care of my son, Adnam Josephus. We will build a new Jerusalem at Avalon".

Taking Mary Magdalene to Safety

Unable to sleep Joseph went on deck to take in the brisk air as the ship moved north, to find Lazarus already sitting on deck. Joseph pulled over a coil of rope and sat next to him. "I know you are worried Lazarus but Mary Magdalene will be safe with her relatives near Marseilles. My ships call at the Port on each return journey to Joppa. The captains will see to it that Mary has everything she needs. Mary's life will be full. After enjoying the reunion with her relatives, Mary will be busy gathering textiles for our ships. How long it will take to mend her broken heart only our God will know".

"Mary loves Marseilles, and the climate there. She travelled many times by ship to Marseilles with her relatives to collect the fine materials used by the women of Galilee in the making of their one piece garments, sought after by traders in the many Ports we travel. Everything is in place for Mary to continue with all the things she loves.

I fear Lazarus that no Port with a Roman Garrison will be completely safe for me to visit at this time. However, I should be beyond the reach of the Temple assassins. I comfort myself with the thought there is much to do now Jesus has gone. Many of our Roman traders will be more interested in the day to day relationships and profiting from their trading businesses, than obeying the will of their distant masters to report on my whereabouts".

Joseph Plans Disciples Missions

I cannot predict at this precise moment Lazarus when it will be safe for me to leave the protection of King Aravagus in Britain, but until that time comes, my ships will transport Disciples from Joppa to Avalon, where I will instruct and disperse them to all the main Ports on our trading routes. I will deposit money and supplies with our close contacts at those ports to enable Disciples to sustain and enlarge their missions".

Dawn was breaking. Lazarus rose to his feet, placed his arm around Joseph's shoulder and gave him a hug. "You are my brother in God. I know your heart was broken into a thousand pieces when you and Nicodemus took Jesus' body whipped and bleeding, from the cross with his legs unbroken, and a wound on his side. You still wear the heartbreak on your face and in your eyes, but soon you will be with your son Adnam at Avalon to whom you have to break the sad news. With Adnam around you, feelings will flow back into your heart".

GLASTONBURY ABBEY RECONSTRUCTED

GLASTONBURY BOWL

68

ST. DAVID AND THE OLD CHURCH

St. David finding the old Church of Glastonbury built by Joseph of Arimathea and his eleven companions, began to build on the Old Church, in honour of these men who knew Jesus and followed Joseph to the Paradise of Avalon.

Many Saints have contributed year by year to this 'Old Church'. St. David being the first Saint to do so.

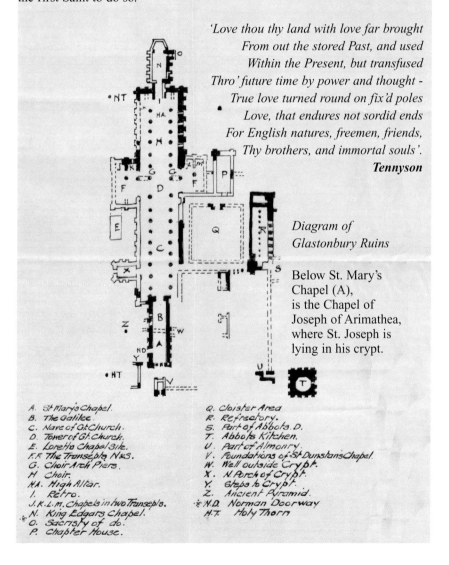

'Love thou thy land with love far brought
From out the stored Past, and used
Within the Present, but transfused
Thro' future time by power and thought -
True love turned round on fix'd poles
Love, that endures not sordid ends
For English natures, freemen, friends,
Thy brothers, and immortal souls'.
Tennyson

Diagram of Glastonbury Ruins

Below St. Mary's Chapel (A), is the Chapel of Joseph of Arimathea, where St. Joseph is lying in his crypt.

A. St Mary's Chapel.
B. The Galilee.
C. Nave of Gt.Church.
D. Tower of Gt.Church.
E. Loretto Chapel Site.
F.F. The Transepts N&S.
G. Choir Arch Piers.
H. Choir.
H.A. High Altar.
I. Retro.
J.K.L.M. Chapels in two Transepts.
N. King Edgars Chapel.
O. Sacristy of do.
P. Chapter House.

Q. Cloister Area.
R. Refractory.
S. Part of Abbots.D.
T. Abbots Kitchen.
U. Part of Almonry.
V. Foundations of St Dunstans Chapel.
W. Well outside Crypt.
X. N Porch of Crypt.
Y. Steps to Crypt.
Z. Ancient Pyramid.
N.D. Norman Doorway.
H.T. Holy Thorn.

IMPORTANT RESEARCH BY THE
REV. R. W. MORGAN IN 1860

My story fits snugly together with the research path and book by Rev. R. W. Morgan confirming beyond doubt, using different historic texts from around the world, the return of Joseph of Arimathea to Glastonbury in AD 38, seeking refuge with his extended family in Cornwall after his expulsion from Judea by the mad Roman Emperor. Not long after his arrival in Cornwall, Joseph went on to build the very first Christian Church outside Jerusalem, at Glastonbury in AD 38. The extensive and comprehensive research by the Rev. Morgan confirms the story beyond any shadow of doubt, the establishment of the very first Christian Church in the world, established in Britain in AD 38, visited by Disciples, all centuries before any missionary or monk arrived from Rome or elsewhere on the shores of any part of Britain.

The Church of Wattle and Daub built by Joseph and his followers remained on the site until it was destroyed by fire in 1184

The fairest way of treating the subject of the first introduction of Christianity into Britain seems to be to lay down an affirmative statement, adduce what evidence there is in support of it, and leave the reader to draw the conclusion whether it makes good such statement or not. We write as investigators, not as dogmatists, but our propositions must of necessity often assume the affirmative form, or we should be mere negationists of history.

Our statement, then, will take the following form : —

Christianity was first introduced into Britain by Joseph of Arimathæa, A.D. 36—39 ; followed by Simon Zelotes, the apostle; then by Aristobulus, the first bishop of the Britons; then by St. Paul. Its first converts were members of the royal family of Siluria—that is, Gladys the sister of Caràdoc, Gladys (Claudia) and Eurgen his daughters, Linus his son, converted in Britain before they were carried into captivity to Rome; then Caràdoc, Brân, and the rest of the family, converted at Rome. The two cradles of Christianity in Britain were Ynys Wydrin, ' the Crystal Isle,' translated by the Saxons Glastonbury, in Somersetshire, where Joseph settled and taught, and Siluria, where the earliest churches and schools, next to Ynys Wydrin, were founded by the Silurian dynasty. Yyns Wydrin was also commonly known as Ynys Avàlon, and in Latin " Domus Dei," " Secretum Dei."

Now for the consecutive evidences of this statement. They have been collected at the cost of much research from various quarters, but the reader will remember that they are not presented as decisive. All historic evidence must be ruled by times and circumstances. If it be such as the times and circumtances of the era alone admit, it is entitled to be received in court, and if there is no contrary evidence which can be brought forward to cancel it, we must bring in, till such evidence be produced, a verdict of proven. The testimony in other historical cases may be stronger and more satisfactory, but we must be content in all cases to give judgment by such evidence as we can command. In ages when literature or written evidence had but very limited existence, tradition and general belief are the chief sources to which we can apply for the knowledge of broad facts, their details being a minor consideration.

The constant current of European tradition affirmed Britain to have been the first country in Europe which received the Gospel, and the British Church to be the most ancient of the Churches of Christ therein. The universality of this opinion is readily demonstrated.

I. Polydore Vergil in the reign of Henry VII., and after him Cardinal Pole (A.D. 1555), both rigid Roman Catholics, affirmed in Parliament, the latter in his address to Philip and Mary, that " Britain was the first of all countries to receive the Christian faith." " The glory of Britain," remarks Genebrard, " consists not only in this, that she was the first country which in a national capacity publicly professed herself Christian, but that she made this confession when the Roman empire itself was Pagan and a cruel persecutor of Christianity."

II. This priority of antiquity was only once questioned, and that on political grounds, by the ambassadors of France and Spain, at the Council of Pisa, A.D. 1417. The Council, however, affirmed it. The ambassadors appealed to the Council of Constance, A.D. 1419, which confirmed the decision of that of Pisa, which was a third time confirmed by the Council of Sena, and then acquiesced in. This decision laid down that the Churches of France and Spain were bound to give way in the points of antiquity and precedency to the Church of Britain, which was founded by Joseph of Arimathæa "immediately after the passion of Christ."[4]

We may therefore accept as the general opinion of Christendom, the priority in point of antiquity over all others of the British Church. This opinion is well expressed by Sabellius:—"Christianity was privately confessed elsewhere, but the first nation that proclaimed it as their religion, and called itself Christian after the name of Christ, was Britain."[5]

It is certain that the primitive British, Irish, Scotch, and Gallic Churches formed one Church, one communion, and that on the assumption of the Papacy, A.D. 606, by Rome, this great Celtic Church, which had been previously in full communion with primitive Rome, refused in the most peremptory

---

[4] "Statim post passionem Christi." An account of the pleadings at the Council of Constance will be found in a thin quarto, *Disceptatio super Dignitatem Angliæ et Galliæ in Concilio Constantiano,* Theod. Martin, (Lovar. 1517).

Robert Parsons, the Jesuit, in his "Three Conversions of England," admits, in common with the great majority of Roman Catholic writers, that Christianity came into Britain direct from Jerusalem. "It seems nearest the truth that the British Church was originally planted by Grecian teachers, such as came from the East, and not by Romans."—Vol. i. p. 15. The Eastern usages of the British Church would alone attest the fact.

[5] Sabell. Enno., lib. vii. c. 5.

I

terms to acknowledge her novel pretensions. It is, of course, this primitive British Church, and not the Roman Church introduced by Augustine, A.D. 596, into Kent among the Pagan Saxons, of which such priority must be understood. That such a Church existed on a national scale, and was thoroughly antagonistic to the Roman Church in its new form and usurpations in the person of Augustine, is so notorious, that we may dispense with all but a few testimonies in proof of the fact. " Britons," declares Bede,[6] " are contrary to the whole Roman world, and enemies to the Roman customs, not only in their Mass, but in their tonsure." The Britons refused to recognise Augustine, or to acquiesce in one of his demands. " We cannot," said the British bishops, " depart from our ancient customs without the consent and leave of our people." Laurentius, the successor of Augustine, speaks yet more bittterly of the antagonism of the Scotch Church :—

" We have found the Scotch bishops worse even than the British. Dagon, who lately came here,

---

6 Bede's Hist. Frag., quoted by Usher, " Ancient Irish Church," c. 4, Hist., lib. ii. c. 2. One demand of Augustine was that the British Church should recognise him as Archbishop. " At illi," says Bede, lib. ii. p. 112, " nihil horum se facturos neque illum pro Archiepiscopo habituros esse respondebant." Bede must himself, one would suppose, from his own testimony in favour of the British Church, and his knowledge of its extent and institutions, have felt some astonishment at this demand of an emissary whose only religious establishment in Britain was a solitary church among the Pagans of Kent. " The Britons," he writes, lib. i. c. 4, " preserved the faith which they had received under King Lucius uncorrupted and entire in peace and tranquillity, until the time of the Emperor Diocletian." Nicholas Trivet says, " Abbot Dionothus, of Bangor, treated Augustine with contempt."

being a bishop of the Scots, refused so much as to eat at the same table, or sleep one night under the same roof with us."[7]

And the protest of the British Church itself, signed on its behalf by the Archbishop of St. David's, six bishops, and the abbot of Bangor, who conducted the conference with Augustine at Augustine's Oak, A.D. 607, place in still clearer light the gulf which the change of the primitive Roman Church into the Papacy formed between the Churches hitherto in full communion. It ran as follows:—

"Be it known and declared that we all, individually and collectively, are in all humility prepared to defer to the Church of God, and to the Bishop of Rome, and to every sincere and godly Christian, so far as to love every one according to his degree, in perfect charity, and to assist them all by word and in deed in becoming the children of God. But as for any other obedience, we know of none that he whom you term the Pope, or Bishop of Bishops, can demand. The deference we have mentioned we are ready to pay to him, as to every other Christian, but in all other respects our obedience is due to the jurisdiction of the Bishop of Caerleon, who is alone, under God, our ruler to keep us right in the way of salvation."[8]

It is plain from these and similar testimonies that Britain—1. Was a distinct diocese of the empire. 2. That it was subject neither to the patriarch of Rome, nor to any foreign ecclesiastical jurisdiction.

---

[7] Laurentii Epist. ad Papam; Bede, Eccles. Hist., ii. c. 4.

[8] Hengwrt MSS.; Humphry Llwyd; Sebright MSS.; Cottonian Library (British Museum), Cleopatra, E. i. 1.

3. That it had its sovereignty within itself. 4. That it never consulted the see of Rome nor any foreign power in its rites, discipline, government, or consecration of bishops and archbishops. 5. That it recognised no superior but God to its archbishop of Caerleon, or St. David.[9]

As late as the twelfth century no instance could be produced of the British metropolitan receiving the pall from Rome.

The two British metropolitans of London and York, Theon and Tediac, had retired from their sees into Wales A.D. 586, ten years only before the arrival of Augustine.

In the Diocletian persecution the British Church supplied the following remarkable list of native martyrs:—Amphibalus, Bishop of Llandaff; Alban of Verulam; Aaron and Julius, presbyters of Caerleon; Socrates, Archbishop of York; Stephen, Archbishop of London; Augulius, his successor; Nicholas, Bishop of Penrhyn (Glasgow); Melior, Bishop of Carlisle, and above 10,000 communicants in different grades of society.

Its religious institutions were on an immense scale. William of Malmesbury describes the ruins of Bangor Iscoed Abbey in his days as those of a city—the most extensive he had seen in the kingdom. Two other British foundations in England retained their superiority over all others of a later date, under every change of rulers till the Re-

---

[9] Spelmanni Concilia; Sir Roger Twysden, Historical Vindication; Brerewood, p. 113; Collier, vol. i. p. 6, &c.; Bishop Lloyd's Government, &c., &c.

formation—St. Alban and Glastonbury. Of all the monasteries these continued the most popular and highly venerated.

Tracing our course back from the Diocletian era, a *consensus* of authorities fixes the national establishment of Christianity in Britain somewhere about the middle of the second century. From A.D. 33, then, to A.D. 150, we have in round numbers a space of 120 years left for the propagation of the faith and the gradual conversion of the nation.

All accounts concur in stating that the person who baptized Lucius, or Lleeuer Mawr, the monarch who thus established the Church, was his uncle, St. Timotheus, the son of Pudens and Claudia, who was brought up on the knees of the apostles.

---

10 It is certain, states Spelman, (p. 18,) that the people of that province held no oath so sacred as that " by the old church " (Glastonbury), fearing nothing so much as to incur the guilt of perjury in taking it. " The church of Glastonbury, from its antiquity called by the Angles ' Ealde Churche,' savoured of sanctity from its very foundation. Here arrive whole tribes of the lower orders, thronging every path. Here, divested of their pomp, assemble the opulent. It has become the crowded residence of the literary and religious. There is no corner of the church in which the ashes of some saint do not repose. The very floor inlaid with polished stones, and the sides of the altar, and even the altar itself, above and beneath, are laden with the multitude of relics. The antiquity, and multitude of saints, have endowed the place with such sanctity that at night scarcely any one presumes to keep vigil there, or during the day to spit upon the floor. St. Patrick is buried by the right side of the altar in the ' old church.' The men of Ireland frequent it to kiss the relics. St. David, that celebrated and incomparable man, built and dedicated the second church here. He sleeps by St. Patrick."—*William of Malmesbury,* b. i. c. 2. St. Aidan was buried by the side of St. David.

The infancy of Timotheus carries us back to Paul himself, to Claudia, to Pudens, to Linus, Caractacus, Brân, and the other members of the Silurian house in their captivity at Rome.

But we have seen that Pudens and others were Christians before Paul came to Rome, which carries the first British conversions to an earlier date than A.D. 58.

And thus we arrive within twenty-five years of the Crucifixion. In which of these years, then, was the Gospel first introduced into Britain?

Gildas, the British historian, who flourished A.D. 520—560, states expressly that it was introduced the last year of the reign of Tiberius Cæsar.[11]

The Crucifixion took place in the seventeenth year of Tiberius. The last year of Tiberius would be his twenty-second. Consequently, if we follow Gildas, Christianity was introduced into Britain five years after the Crucifixion, that is, A.D. 38.

This is certainly an early period, but Gildas speaks positively,—"ut scimus." It synchronizes with the first persecution of the Church by Saul of Tarsus, and its general dispersion. "They were all scattered abroad except the apostles."[12] If all, then Joseph of Arimathæa among them. Regarding Gildas' date as our starting-point, we have the following testimonies assigning the introduction of Christianity in or about the same year to Joseph of Arimathæa:—

1. Gregory of Tours, in his History of the

---

[11] "We know that Christ, the true Sun, afforded His light to our island in the last year of Tiberius Cæsar."— "Tempore ut scimus, summo Tiberii Cæsaris."—*Histor. Briton.* Usher terms Gildas "auctor veracissimus."

[12] Acts viii. 1.

Franks:[13] He flourished *circiter* A.D. 544—595. This is Gallic testimony.

2. The Pseudo-Gospel of Nicodemus,[14] supposed to be a composition of the fourth century. This is Oriental tradition.

3. Maelgwyn of Llandaff, the uncle of St. David. His era is *circiter* A.D. 450. His words being remarkable, we insert them at length:—" Joseph of Arimathæa, the noble decurion, received his everlasting rest with his eleven associates in the Isle of Avàlon. He lies in the southern angle of the bifurcated line of the Oratorium of the Adorable Virgin. He has with him the two white vessels of silver which were filled with the blood and the sweat of the great Prophet Jesus.[15]"

This is British testimony, of one also personally acquainted with the interior of the church of Avàlon, or Domus Dei, and the exact spot within it of the resting-place of Joseph. The greater weight is due to Maelgwyn's evidence, as no fact is better established than the reconstruction of the Domus Dei

---

13 P. 133.   14 Ad finem.

15 " Joseph ab Arimathea nobilis decurio in insula Avalloniâ cum xi. Sociis suis somnum cepit perpetuum et jacet in meridiano angulo lineæ bifurcatæ Oratorii Adorandæ Virginis. Habet enim secum duovascula argentea alba cruore et sudore magni prophetæ Jesu perimpleta."—Thick vellum Cottonian MS., quoted also by Usher, *Melchini Fragmentum*. Joseph of Arimathæa is by Eastern tradition said to have been the younger brother of the father of the Virgin Mary. The records of Glastonbury, as cited by Malmesbury and others, preserved the genealogy of his descendants in Britain :—" Helias nepos Joseph genuit Josua, Josua genuit Amminadab, Amminadab Castellor," &c.—*Historia de Glastonbury*.

on a cathedral scale by his nephew, St. David the Archbishop.[16]

4. The Vatican manuscript, quoted by Baronius in his "Ecclesiastical Annals," *ad annum* 35, (the same year in which the Acts of the Apostles state all, except the apostles, were scattered abroad from Judæa). The manuscript records that in this year Lazarus, Maria Magdalene, Martha, her handmaiden Marcella, Maximin a disciple, Joseph the Decurion of Arimathæa, against all of whom the Jewish people had special reasons of enmity, were exposed to the sea in a vessel without sails or oars. The vessel drifted finally to Marseilles, and they were saved. From Marseilles Joseph and his company passed into Britain, and after preaching the Gospel there, died.[17]

5. The *Chronicon* of Pseudo-Dexter, the *Fragmenta* of Haleca Archbishop of Saragossa, Frecul-

---

[16] In the two "vascula argentea alba," full of the Saviour's blood and sweat shed on the cross and at Gethsemane, we have the first nucleus of the celebrated legenda and quest of the Sant-Greal. They gave the name of the Crystal Isle to Glastonbury. The Britons commemorate (writes Forcatulus) that Joseph brought with him the pledge and testimony of the sacred Eucharist, namely, the chalice which was used by the Saviour, and placed before His most holy guests the apostles, and which is preserved by them (the Britons) as the pledge of the safety of Britain, as the palladium was of that of Troy.— *Forcatulus de Gallor. Imperio et Philos.*, lib. vii. p. 989. *Greal* in British is a collection of elements; *Sant-Greal*, the holy elements.

[17] The respective dates of A.D. 35 and 38 allow three years between the expulsion of Joseph from Judæa and his settlement in Britain—an undesigned harmony which goes far chronologically to confirm the common record.

phus and Forcatulus,[18] deliver the same statement professedly from primitive sources of unknown date. Cressy, Pitsæus, Sanders, Alford, the Roman Catholic historians, concur with Gildas in the year, and with the above authorities in holding Joseph of Arimathæa to have been the first who preached Christ in Britain.

6. We possess abundant proofs that Britain was studded with Christian churches before the end of the second century, and whatever direction our investigations take, we find authorities unanimous in the statement that the church of Joseph in Avàlon, or Glastonbury, was the first and oldest of these churches, many affirming it to be the oldest or senior Christian church in the whole world. It will be useful to transcribe the conclusions arrived at by the historians who have treated on this subject before us.

" The church of Avàlon in Britain no other hands than those of the disciples of the Lord themselves built."—*Publius Discipulus.*

" The mother church of the British Isles is the Church in Insula Avallonia, called by the Saxons Glaston."—*Usher.*

" If credit be given to ancient authors, this church of Glastonbury is the senior church of the world."—*Fuller.*

" It is certain that Britain received the faith in the first age from the first sowers of the Word. Of all the churches whose origin I have investigated in Britain, the church of Glastonbury is the most ancient."—*Sir Henry Spelman.*

Had any doubt existed on this point of priority, it certainly would have been contested by some other

---

[18] Lib. vii. p. 989.

church in our island, for it was not a question of mere chronology, but one which drew with it enormous privileges and advantages. It never was disputed. It was universally conceded: and upon it the long series of the royal charters of the church and monastery, from that of King Arthur, the nephew of its second founder, St. David, to that of Edward III., proceed. "The first church in the kingdom, built by the disciples of Christ," says the charter of Edgar. "This is the city," states the charter of Ina, or Ivor, "which was the fountain and origin of Christ's religion in Britain, built by Christ's disciples."

The tombs of Saxon and British kings, saints, bishops, and abbots, buried in and around its confines, confirm the charters.

Of the general truth of the Arimathæan mission there have been numerous supporters. No author, indeed, who has taken due pains to examine its evidences, rejects its main facts. "We dare not deny," writes the caustic Fuller, "the substance of the story." Bishop Godwin, in his quaint style, writes, "The testimonies of Joseph of Arimathæa's coming here are so many, so clear, and so pregnant, as an indifferent man cannot but discern there is something in it.[19]" Archbishop Usher defends it with his usual display of erudition, and with unusual vehemency of manner, as if the honour of ecclesiastical Britain rested on its truth. The reader will form his own judgment.

For our part, we cast aside the addenda and crescenda, the legends, poems, marvels which after ages, monk, troubadour, and historian piled high and

---

[19] Godwin's "Catalogue of Bishops," Præsul., p. 11.

gorgeously on the original foundation. That foundation must indeed have originally possessed no mean strength, depth, and solidity, to bear the immense superstructure which mediæval superstition and literature emulated each other in erecting above the simple tomb of the Arimathæan senator in the Avàlon isle. This superstition was rising tide-high in the time of Augustine, A.D. 600. "In the western confines of Britain," he writes to the Pope, "there is a certain royal island of large extent, surrounded by water, abounding in all the beauties of nature and necessaries of life. In it the first neophytes of the catholic law, God beforehand acquainting them, found a Church constructed by no human art, but by the hands of Christ Himself, for the salvation of His people. The Almighty has made it manifest by many miracles and mysterious visitations that He continues to watch over it as sacred to Himself, and to Mary the mother of God."[20] The same edifice of figments has been built in all ages, more or less, on Christianity itself, but we do not therefore demur to the primitive facts of Christianity. Leaving details out of the question, the cardinal features of the first, or Arimathæan, mission of Christianity into Britain are, in our opinion, entitled to historic acceptance and registration.

These cardinal features we consider to be the following:—Joseph and his company, including Lazarus, Mary, Martha, Marcella, and Maximin, came at the invitation of certain Druids of high rank,[21] from

---

[20] Epistolæ ad Gregorium Papam.

[21] " Negotium habuit cum Druidis quorum primi precipuique doctores erant in Britannia."—*Freculphus, apud God.*, p. 10.

Marseilles into Britain, *circiter* A.D. 38, 39; were located at Ynys Avàlon, the seat of a Druidic cor, which was subsequently made over to them in free gift by Arviragus. Here they built the first church, which became the centre and mother of Christianity in Britain. Here also they terminated their mortal career, the gentle and conciliatory character of Joseph securing the protection of the reigning family, and the conversion of many of its members. Joseph died and was interred A.D. 76.

The church was 60 ft. in length by 26 in breadth, built *Gallico more* of timber pillars and framework doubly wattled inside and out, and thatched with straw.[22] This simplicity might have been the effect of necessity or design. The Druidic faith required three essentials in every temple :—1. It must be circular; 2. Hypæthral, or roofless at top, and open at the sides; 3. Its materials must be monoliths, vast single stones unhewed, untouched by metal. The Arimathæan church rose in direct though humble antagonism to the old Cyclopean architecture—it was oblong, it was of wood, it was roofed and covered in. The Druidic mind could not, without a strong effort, connect such a building with the ideas of religion and worship. It carried with it no image, no symbolism of the One, the Infinite, and the Darkless. The Briton on his way to one of the great cors—Amesbury or Stonehenge, with their miles of obelisks—would smile with pity on the *ecclesia*, or, as he rendered this new word from the

---

[22] And such also was the primitive Capitol of Rome :—
" Quæ fuerat nostri si quæras Regia nati,
   Adspice de Canna straminibusque Domum."
              Ovid, Fast. ad Fest. Roma.

84

East, the *eglwys* of the *Wyr Israel*, (men of Israel).
But the Druidic religion knew of no such monstrous
abortions as intolerance and persecution. There is no
instance of Druidism persecuting conscience or knowledge. Such crime was left for Rome, for a religion
of foreign importation. Casting his eye round the
circle of the horizon, and then upwards to the vast
open dome of heaven, the Briton saw the outer ring,
as it were, the circumference of his own Druidic
cor: he would resume his march, trying to discover
some possible identification in nature between an oblong pitched roof and the temple of the universe.

The tomb of Joseph was inscribed with the following epitaph, touching from its spirit of faith, peace,
and humility:—[23]

" AD BRITANNOS VENI POST CHRISTUM SEPELIVI.
DOCUI. QUIEVI."

Of the perpetual exemption of the twelve ploughs
of land conferred by Arviragus on the Arimathæan
Church, the Domesday Survey of A.D. 1088 supplies
curious confirmation. " The Domus Dei, in the
great monastery of Glastingbury, called the Secret
of the Lord. This Glastingbury church possesses,
in its own villa, xii. hides of land which have never
paid tax."[1]

After A.D. 35—36 Joseph disappears from the
Scripture narrative.

---

[23] Hearne's Antiquities of Glastonbury; Leland, ibid.;
John of Tynemouth, Ad Josephum Arimath.

[1] " Domus Dei in magno Glaston. monasterio quod
secretum Domini vocatur, Ecclesia Glaston. habet in ipsa
villa xii. hydas quæ nunquam geldaverunt."—*Domesday
Survey,* fol., p. 449.

The Greek and Roman menologies and Martyrologies commemorate with scrupulous jealousy the obituaries and death-places of all the earlier Christian characters of mark who died within the pale of the Roman empire. They nowhere record those of Joseph. Now we know from Tertullian that Britain was Christian before it was Roman. The Dove conquered where the Eagle could make no progress. "Regions in Britain which have never been penetrated by the Roman arms," are his words, (A.D. 192) "have received the religion of Christ." If this statement were correct, after the war between Rome and Britain had raged for a century and a half, from A.D. 43 to A.D. 192—and in a national point of view it is impartial testimony, for Tertullian was an African—it is obvious that the Arimathæan mission must have been founded in the heart of independent Britain, quite out of the pale, therefore, of the Roman empire. And this inference tallies with the rest of the evidence. Joseph died in these *loca inaccessa Romanis*. His death, therefore, could not be chronicled by Greek or Roman Churches.

Lazarus is asserted to have accompanied Joseph. The only record we possess of him beyond the Scripture narrative[2] is in a very ancient British Triad : "The Triad of Lazarus, the three counsels of Lazarus : Believe in God who made thee; Love God who saved thee; Fear God who will judge thee."[3] It is difficult to explain how the name and counsel of Lazarus could find their way into these peculiarly

---

[2] The tradition of the Church of Lyons makes him return with Martha and Mary to Marseilles, of which town he became the first bishop, and there died.

[3] Triads of Primitive Britain.

British memorials except by his presence and teaching in Britain.

Finally, were there any other eminent converts, besides those of the Silurian family, made at this very early date in Britain? Three are particularly mentioned—Beatus, whose first name was Suetonius, Mansuetus, and Marcellus.

Beatus, born of noble parents in Britain, was there also converted and baptized. He became the founder of the Helvetian Church. He fixed his mission at Underseven, on the lake of Thun, disposing of all his property to ransom prisoners of war. His death occurred in the cell still shown at Underseven, A.D. 96.[4]

Mansuetus, born in Hibernia, converted and baptized in Britain, was sent afterwards from Rome with St. Clement, afterwards the second bishop of Rome, to preach the Gospel in Gaul. He founded the Lotharingian Church, fixing his mission at Toul, where, after extending his labours to Illyria, he suffered martyrdom, A.D. 110.[5]

Marcellus, a noble Briton, became bishop of Tongres, and afterwards founder-bishop of Treves—the diocese which for centuries exercised the chief influence in the Gallic Church. The conversion of Linus, the son of Caractacus, is attributed to him.[6]

---

4 Theatr. Magn. Britan., lib. vi. p. 9.

5 Pantaleon, De Viris Illus. Germaniæ, pars. I.; Guliel. Eisengren, cent. 2, p. 5; Petrus Mersæus, De Sanctis German.; Franciscus Guilliman, Helvetiorum Historia, lib. i. c. 15; Petrus de Natalibus, Episcop. Regal. Tallensis.

6 Marcellus Britannus, Tungrorum episcopus postea Trevirorum Archiepiscopus," &c.—*Mersæus, De Archiepiscopis Trevirensium.*

Before, therefore, the incorporation of Britain with the Roman empire, whilst the war of invasion raged, we have before us these remarkable facts:—1. A young and vigorous Christian Church, direct from Jerusalem and the East, and which had never touched or passed through Rome, was in full and successful work in the heart of independent Britain, under the protection of the very sovereign and family that conducted the war against Rome. 2. This native Church, though so young, does not limit its operations to Britain. It ramifies from Britain to the Continent, and becomes, through native-born missionaries, the mother-Church of Gaul, Lotha-ingia, and Helvetia. Providence, for the most part, works in a very noiseless way, by natural means. Nothing could be more natural than that Joseph and his companions,—for whom, as Christians, there was neither peace nor safety among their own country-men; for whom, as Christians and Jews, there was no assurance of their lives in any Roman province,—should seek refuge in the only independent kingdom of the West, whose national religion, like their own, was marked for destruction on the Continent; for, as we have seen, the decrees of Augustus, Tiberius, and Claudius constituted Druidism a capital offence.[7] Nothing could be more natural than that Guiderius and Aviragus, on the intercession of influential Druids, should receive and protect such refugees, and in accordance with their own Druidic principles, leave whatever religion they professed to the volun-tary acceptance or rejection of their subjects. All this, we repeat, was very natural, yet we may well

---

[7] " Penitus religionem Druidarum abolevit Claudius."— *Suetonius, in Vitâ Claud.*

affirm that Providence was working in the wheel of Nature. If the stoker was Nature, the engineer was Providence. Under this reflection lies another. Whatever the errors of Druidism were, it was, in its main truths, a grand religion, forming grand and truthful characters. Its foundation-maxim was, "Truth against the world"; literally, against " all being."[8]

Now, if we just cast our eye on Britain, on a Druidic Caractacus, Arviragus, or Claudia, listening from their thrones to a Christian missionary, because he professed to bring and to preach truth, and Christ as the Truth, the Way, and the Life; then cast the other on a Pilate, asking, in the profoundest disbelief in all virtue and goodness, " What is truth?" we shall see at a glance that Britain was prepared, and the Roman empire not prepared, for Christianity. The British and Roman minds were different. Druidism, therefore, dissolved by the natural action of its own principles into Christianity. No persecution until the tenth, under Diocletian, touched Britain, for Christianity had become nationality. And the Diocletian was stopped in two years, on his own responsibility, at the hazard of civil war, by Constantius. Then rose Constantine, with a British army sworn to put down the persecution of Christianity for ever. The clue is a national, a British one.

The next missionary after Joseph was Simon Zelotes the apostle. There can be little doubt, we think, on this point. One Menology assigns the

---

[8] St. Paul's maxim, " We can do nothing against the truth," breathes a kindred spirit, and would at once conciliate a Druidic hearer.

K

martyrdom of Zelotes to Persis in Asia, but others agree in stating he suffered in Britain. Of these the principal authority is Dorotheus, Bishop of Tyre, in the reigns of Diocletian and Constantius, (A.D. 300). His testimony we consider decisive:—" Simon Zelotes traversed all Mauritania, and the regions of the Africans, preaching Christ. He was at last crucified, slain, and buried in Britain."[9] Crucifixion was a Roman penalty for runagate slaves, deserters, and rebels: it was not known to the British laws. We conclude Simon Zelotes suffered in the east of Britain, perhaps, as tradition affirms, in the vicinity of Caistor, under the prefecture of Caius Decius, the officer whose atrocities were the immediate cause of the Boadicean war. Two things strike the investigator of early Christian history: the marvellous manner in which Christian seed is found growing and fructifying in unheard-of places; the indifference of the sowers to perpetuating their own name and labours. They seem to have been quite satisfied and blest in sowing Christ, and then resting. The epitaph of Joseph of Avàlon would express the feelings of all:—*Docui, Quievi,* ' I taught, I have entered on my rest.' Beautiful as is this in fact and faith, it is very unsatisfactory in history. As Christians we feel its propriety; as writers we desiderate more of that yearning for immortality on earth which inspires the Greek and Latin authors, and inspires us also in reading them. Yet the effects of the Christian principle are undoubtedly greater; for the principle it is which meets us face to face. It is Christ or self. We come on a field: the sower has inclosed it, built round it strongly, sowed proved

---

[9] Dorotheus, Synod. de Apostol. ; Synopsis ad Sim Zelot.

seed in it, entrusted it to a few like-minded men, and he vanishes. He is crucified a thousand miles off, leaves no memoir of himself, no message to posterity, no foot-mark on the geology of the Church. In perusing the Apostolic Epistles we are struck by the maximum of censure, the minimum of approval conveyed to the Churches. We are apt to think they had little force or vitality. But when we extend our survey to the whole empire of Rome, we are almost terrified at the subterraneous shocks with which these Churches are everywhere bringing Pagan temple and tower to the ground. We try to calculate and value this power. We fail in doing it. The Roman government failed also. It is an unknown power, the source of which is from above.

3. Next to Jospeh and Simon Zelotes came Aristobulus. " It is perfectly certain," writes Alford,[10] " that before St. Paul had come to Rome Aristobulus was absent in Britain." We have seen he was not at Rome when Paul wrote his Epistle. Now Aristobulus must have been far advanced in years, for he was the father-in-law of St. Peter. His wife was the subject of the miracle recorded by St. Matthew. His daughter bore Peter a son and a daughter. We have the following evidences that he preached the Gospel and was martyred in Britain :—

The Martyrologies of the Greek Churches :— " Aristobulus was one of the seventy disciples, and

---

10 Alford's Regia Fides, vol. i. p. 83. Alford, whose proper name was Griffiths, and who assumed the name of Alford on entering the Society of Jesuits, is, next to Baronius, the most learned of the Roman Catholic historians. His *Regia Fides* is a wonderful monument of erudition and research.

a follower of St. Paul the Apostle, along with whom he preached the Gospel to the whole world, and ministered to him. He was chosen by St. Paul to be the missionary bishop to the land of Britain, inhabited by a very warlike and fierce race. By them he was often scourged, and repeatedly dragged as a criminal through their towns, yet he converted many of them to Christianity. He was there martyred, after he had built churches and ordained deacons and priests for the island."[11]

Haleca, Bishop of Augusta, to the same effect:— "The memory of many martyrs is celebrated by the Britons, especially that of St. Aristobulus, one of the seventy disciples."[12]

Dorotheus, A.D. 303:—"Aristobulus, who is mentioned by the Apostle in his Epistle to the Romans, was made bishop in Britain."[13]

Adonis Martyrologia:—"Natal day of Aristobulus, Bishop of Britain, brother of St. Barnabas the Apostle, by whom he was ordained bishop. He was sent to Britain, where, after preaching the truth of Christ and forming a Church, he received martyrdom."[14]

The British *Achau*, or Genealogies of the Saints of Britain:—"These came with Brân the Blessed from Rome to Britain—Arwystli Hên (*Senex*), Ilid, Cyndaw, men of Israel; Maw, or Manaw, son of Arwystli Hên."[15]

According to the genius of the British tongue, Aristobulus becomes Arwystli.

---

[11] Greek Men., ad 15 March.
[12] Halecæ Fragments in Martyr.
[13] Synopsis ad Aristobulum.
[14] In Diem Martii 17.   [15] Achau Saint Prydain.

A district in Montgomeryshire, on the Severn, perpetuates by its name (Arwystli) the scene of his martyrdom.

The Britons must have had Arwystli in person among them; they must have been struck by the age of the venerable missionary, or the epithet *Senex* would not have become amongst them part of his name.

There are several points here to be noted. The first is, that Aristobulus was sent into Britain by St. Paul before St. Paul came himself to Rome, and even before the Epistle to the Romans was written, for Aristobulus, when St. Paul wrote it, had left for his mission. The large space given by the Roman historians to the wars in Britain demonstrates the interest felt in them by the whole empire. Britain was a familiar term in every household. Upon it the whole military attention had for some years been concentrated. The name of Arviragus had by this time attained as great a celebrity as that of his cousin Caractacus—it was in every one's mouth; and Juvenal could suggest no news which would have been hailed by the Roman people with more intense satisfaction than that of his fall : —

> " Hath our great enemy
> Arviragus, the car-borne British king,
> Dropped from his battle-throne ? "

It is certain, therefore, that St. Paul, who travelled everwhere, mixing with every kind of society, must have been as well acquainted with Britain, and the events passing therein, as any other intelligent Roman citizen. There was everything to attract his eye to it as a field for Gospel labour and enterprise.

But have we any Scripture evidence that St. Paul at this time thought at all of Western Europe? Undoubtedly we have. Commentators and writers of his life generally refer to his visit to Spain as contemplated after his first imprisonment at Rome. A reference to the passage in the fifteenth chapter of the Epistle shows, on the contrary, that his journey to Spain was meditated not only before he came to Rome, but that it was his principal object in leaving the East, his call at Rome being simply by the way. " Whensoever I take my journey into Spain, I will come to you, for I trust to see you on my journey, and to be brought on my way thitherward by you."[16] He speaks of the journey as a thing decided upon, taking Rome by the way. Literally, in the original it is, " I hope in passing through to see you." It was the West of Europe, then, beyond Rome, not Rome itself, which was the Apostle's mark, even at this comparatively early date. All the incidents and delays which occurred between this date (A.D. 56), and the termination of his first imprisonment at Rome, were interruptions of his original plan of operations. His destination was the extreme West, and this was in accordance with the command of Christ, " I will send thee *far* hence to the Gentiles." According to the Scriptures, therefore, and the view we have therein of Paul's own mind, we think we are justified in concluding that having already sent Aristobulus into Britain, he intended to traverse Spain himself, and thence join his fellow-labourer in our island; for it is plain that Aristobulus acted as wholly under Paul's instructions in Britain as Titus in Crete or Timothy in Asia Minor. " He preached

---

[16] Rom. xv. 24.

the Gospel with St. Paul to the whole world, and ministered to him."[17]

It appears that Brân left Rome with Aristobulus, his son Manaw, Ilid, and Cyndaw, before Caràdoc. He was accompanied also by Eurgain, the eldest daughter of Caràdoc, and her husband Salog, lord in her right of Caer Salog, (Salisbury,) a Roman patrician. Ilid established his mission under the protection of Brân, his grandson Cyllinus, (eldest son of Caràdoc,) Salog and Eurgain, in the centre of Siluria, on the spot in Glamorganshire known from that period till the present as Llan-Ilid. At this *Llan*, or 'consecrated inclosure,' the Princess Eurgain founded and endowed the first Christian cor, or choir, in Britain. From this Cor-Eurgain issued many of the most eminent teachers and missionaries of Christianity down to the tenth century. Of the saints of this cor, from Ilid in succession, there are catalogues in the "Genealogies of the Saints of Britain."[18]

Eastern and Western testimonies concur in thus proving the Aristobulian mission to Britain under the Sanction of Brân and his family. We complete the chain with the two following, from historic sources : —

"The three blessed sovereigns of the isle of Bri-

---

[17] Greek Menology, ad Diem Martii 17.

[18] Achau Saint Prydain. In these *Achau*, or genealogies, Eurgain is commemorated as the first female saint of the isle of Britain. Her conversion, therefore, preceded that of her sister Claudia. Ilid was a Hebrew :—
    " Hast thou heard the saying of Ilid,
    One come of the race of Israel?
    ' There is no mania like passion.' "—
                                    British Proverbs.

tain:—1. Brân, son of Llyr Llediaith, who first brought the faith of Christ to the Cymry from Rome, where he had been seven years a hostage for his son Caràdoc, whom the Romans put in prison, after being betrayed by the plotting, deceit and enticement of Arèddig. 2. Lleuver, or Leirwg, (Lucius,) son of Coel, son of St. Cyllin, son of Caràdoc, son of Brân, son of Llyr Llediaith, called Lleuver the Great, who founded the first church of Llandaff, and first gave the privileges of the country and nation to all who professed the faith in Christ. 3. Cadwalladr the Blessed, who gave protection within all his lands to the Christians who fled from the pagan Saxons who wished to slay them."[19]

"The three priorities of the Cymry:—1. Priority as the first colonizers of Britain; 2. Priority of government and civilization; 3. Priority as the first Christians of Britain."[20]

In an ancient collection of British proverbs we find certain sayings transmitted of Brân and the first Christians of Britain:—

> "Hast thou heard the saying of Ilid,
> The saint of the race of Israel?
> 'No folly but ends in misery.'
>
> Hast thou heard the saying of the noble Brân,
> The blessed, to all the renowned?
> 'There is no good but God Himself.'
>
> Hast thou heard the saying of Caràdoc,
> The exalted son of the noble Brân?
> 'Oppression persisted in brings on death.' "

We have at this stage of the inquiry two distinct cradles of Christianity in Britain,—the mission of Joseph in Avàlon, and the Cor-Eurgain at Llan-Ilid

---

[19] Triads of the isle of Britain.   [20] Triads of the Cymry.

96

in Wales; the former protected by Arviragus, the
latter fostered by the family of Caràdoc, his cousin.
We can entertain no reasonable doubt that very in-
timate ties bound these two Christian missions together. St. Barnabas, Aristobulus his brother, and
Joseph were members of the Jerusalem Church—
they were of the one hundred and twenty which
constituted it prior to the day of Pentecost—the
same spiritual union, the same friendship, the same
one faith, one heart, one mind, one baptism, one
hope, one Lord, would join them together in Britain
as in Jerusalem.   Both establishments were out of
the pale of Rome, both among the free states of
Britain.   Beyond Siluria, among the Ordovices, the
protection of Brân did not avail Aristobulus : Joseph
came direct from Jerusalem, and was therefore regarded with favour; Aristobulus came from Rome,
from the metropolis of the national enemy, and fell,
perhaps, rather a victim to this fact than a martyr
to religion.   In Siluria itself the royal family were
hard pressed to reconcile their subjects to the presence of men in any way, however slightly, connected with Rome, so unappeasable was the hatred
borne to the invaders, so easily misapprehended and
confounded every embassage from their city.   Every
overture of peace made by the Roman government
to this *ferox provincia* was sternly rejected; rigour
and mildness were alike thrown away.   " The race
of the Silures," observes Tacitus, "was not to be
changed by clemency or severity."[21]   Even after the
treaty which incorporated Britain with Rome, (A.D.
118,) two-thirds of the whole military force of the

---

[21] " Silurum gens non atrocitate, non clementiâ muta-
batur."—*Taciti Annal,* lib. ii. c. 24.

island continued to be stationed on the frontiers of Wales, at Chester and Caeleon. The same dogged opposition to the foreigner characterised the same race in the West in the later Saxon eras. " It is certain," writes Kemble, " that neither Roman nor Saxon produced any effect worth mentioning on the Cymric race and language west of the Severn. We see indeed what little effect all the centuries since then, though but a river divides the two races, has produced upon the British language."[22]

Great caution, therefore, was called for in the exercise, under these circumstances, of the royal protection. Meanwhile, however, the cor continued to strike roots. The royal family themselves remained firm in the profession of Christianity. Cyllinus, who acted as regent in the absence of his father Caràdoc, had all his children baptized. Converts increased, and more teachers arrived from Greece and Rome. The following notice of St. Cyllinus is extracted from the family records of Jestyn ap Gwrgant, Prince of Glamorgan, in the eleventh century :—

" Cyllin ab Caràdog, a wise and just king. In his days many of the Cymry embraced the faith in Christ through the teaching of the saints of Cor-Eurgain, and many godly men from the countries of

---

[22] History of the Anglo-Saxons, vol. i. Tacitus, in his Life of Agricola (c. 21), takes occasion to notice the stubborn attachment of the Briton to his native tongue. And it is one of the most remarkable facts connected with the occupation of Britain by the Romans, that though they entirely recast the languages of the Continent through the medium of their own, they did not leave probably a hundred Latin words behind them in Britain : within twenty years of their departure Latin had ceased to be spoken in the island.

Greece and Rome were in Cambria. He first of the Cymry gave infants names; for before, names were not given except to adults, and then from something characteristic in their bodies, minds, or manners."[23] Nero had succeeded Claudius Sept. 2ծ, A.D. 53. He was in his seventeenth year, and for some time remained under the influence of Seneca, a Stoic philosopher in profession but in practice a grinding usurer. The capital of this minister amounted to fifteen million pounds sterling of modern money. Two millions of this he advanced to the Iceni of Britain on the security of their public buildings. We doubt if Rothschild or any modern capitalist would advance half the sum on such buildings as may now be found in the old Icenic counties. The king of the Iceni was Prasutagus, his queen Victoria (in British, Vuddig or Boeddig—Boadicea). Tacitus speaks of him as a sovereign whose wealth was notorious at Rome,—*longâ clarus opulentiâ.*

The commerce between Britain and the Continent continued to be vigorously conducted. Tacitus informs us that the great foreign emporium was London, a city the foundation of which the British annals carried back 270 years before that of Rome, i.e., B.C. 1020.[1] Above 80,000 Roman citizens, ac-

[23] Gwehelyth Iestyn ap Gwrgant.
[1] " Londinum vetus oppidum quod Augustam posteritas appellavit."—*Ammianus Marcellinus,* lib. xxvii. c. 8, 9. If London was not a præ-Roman city, Ammianus could not term it " an ancient city :" for supposing it founded the first year of the Claudian invasion, A.D. 43, it would still, in A.D. 350, be quite a new town ; and as the Boadicean war broke out A.D. 60, it would be absurd to affirm that it rose in seventeen years to the condition described by Tacitus : " Copiâ negotiatorum et commeatuum maxime celebre."—*Tacit. Annal.,* lib. i. ; *Hist.,* lib. i., and lib. xiv. c. 27—30.

cording to the Roman historians, perished in the Boadicean war, of whom the greater number resided in London. A Roman garrison stationed in the Prætorium,—which extended along the Thames from the temple of Diana, where now stands St. Paul's, to the Bryn Gwyn, or White Mount, the site of the Tower, —protected their property and interests. It was just as easy for an apostle to find his way into Britain as for any of these 80,000, amongst whom there must have been a fair proportion of Christians. The Roman citizen could travel from Babylon to London along the great military *itinera* of the empire, more slowly indeed, but with fewer civil inconveniences in the shape of passports and stoppages, and no less security, than an Englishman can now. It was not in mediæval Europe, divided amongst a thousand independent marauding states and barons, nor in the pathless wilds of a new world, but over the length and breadth of an empire possessed of a system of roads laid down with consummate engineering skill, and remaining, until the invention of railroads, without rivals on a great scale, that the first preachers of the Gospel had to travel. The Roman *iter* at Babylon would conduct them, under the protection of one law, one government, without a frontier, to Calais. The whole empire was a network of connected arteries, along which a traveller might take his ease from anywhere to anywhere under the overshadowing protection of the Eagles of the Cæsars. It was not till he had crossed the British Channel that the din and terror of war assaulted his senses. So profound, indeed, until the brief civil commotion that resulted in placing the Vespasian family on the throne, was the peace which prevailed through Europe, that the Roman annalists are driven, for lack of national events, to fill page after page with court scandals, with the personal debaucheries and cruelties of the emperors. These emperors were despots created by the democracy against the oligarchy; they held the same position as the Tudors of later times in Britain. When a noble raised his head above his fellows, like Tarquin and the poppies, they cut it remorselessly and unscrupulously down. A lover of the old oligarchic times, such as Tacitus, would—and no doubt in many cases justly—stigmatize such executions as judicial murders, and transmit their authors to the execration of posterity. The people at large were unaffected; the lightning passed over them; and, in return, it was the dagger of the oligarch in the chamber, not the popular tumult, which the Cæsar dreaded. He walked the streets a simple citizen without guards, but he went to the Senate armed. Meanwhile, Ostorius Scapula in Britain suffered a defeat from Arviragus at Caervèlin, near Caerleon. Exhausted in mind and body by the harassing vicissitudes of the war, he petitioned to be recalled. He was succeeded by Didius Gallus, who founded Cardiff, still called by the Welsh *Caer Dydd*, ' the Castle of Didius.' After a short command Didius gave way to Veranius, under whom the Roman armies were again driven behind the Plautian line of fortresses, and their head-quarters fixed at Verulam. Veranius was superseded by Suetonius Paulinus, a second Fabius Cunctator, and regarded as the ablest tactician in the Roman service.[2] He had under him the ninth, fourteenth, twentieth (Vicesima Valens Victrix), and second (Augusta) legions.

---

[2] " Cunctator naturâ, nemo rei militaris callidior habebatur."—*Taciti Hist.*, lib. xiv. c. 20.

CONCLUSION.

FROM the preceding investigation ensue the following conclusions: —

1. Before Christianity originated in Judæa, there had existed from the remotest period in Britain a religion known as the Druidic, of which the two leading doctrines were identical with those of Christianity, viz., the immortality of the soul and vicarious atonement.

2. That this identity pointed out Britain as of all Gentile countries the one best prepared for the reception of Christianity.

3. That the only religions persecuted by the Roman government were the Druidic and the Christian.

4. That this common persecution by the great military empire with which Britain was engaged in incessant hostilities from A.D. 43 to A.D. 118, materially aided in pre-disposing the British mind in favour of Christianity.

5. That Britain, being the only free state of Europe, was the only country which afforded a

---

bered he is a canonized saint in the Roman calendar— expressly states that the remains of the bodies of the apostles Peter and Paul, the martyrs St. Lawrence, St. John, St. Gregory, and St. Pancras, were, at the solicitation of King Oswy to Pope Vitalian, removed from Rome to England, and deposited at Canterbury A.D. 656, Pope Vitalian's letter to Oswy being extant.—(*Bedæ Hist.*, lib. iii. c. 29.) Their remains, then, if any, repose in British soil.

secure asylum to the Christians persecuted by the Roman government.

6. That a current of Christianity flowed into Britain from the East contemporaneously with the first dispersion of the Church at Jerusalem, A.D. 35—38.

7. That the first planters of the Gospel in Britain never were in Rome at all, but came hither from the mother Church at Jerusalem.

8. That these first planters were Joseph of Arimathæa and his associates, who settled under the protection of the British king Arviragus, in the Isle of Avàlon, Glastonbury,—one of the Druidic cors of Somerset.

9. That among the earliest converts of Joseph and his fraternity were Gladys (Pomponia Græcina) the sister, Gladys or Claudia, and Eurgain, the daughters, and Linus the son of Caractacus, prince of Siluria, and military dictator of the national forces against the Romans.

10. That the second planter of the word was Simon Zelotes the apostle, who was martyred and buried in the Roman province, probably near Caistor, in Lincolnshire.

11. That the third planter was Aristobulus, one of the seventy, brother of St. Barnabas and father-in-law of St. Peter; commissioned first bishop of Britain by St. Paul, and consecrated by St. Barnabas, the two apostles to the Gentiles. That Aristobulus was engaged in his mission in Britain when St. Paul wrote his Epistle to the Romans, some years before his first visit, or the visit of any other apostle, to Rome.

12. That Pudens, the husband of Claudia, Claudia herself, her sister Eurgain, her brother Linus, and aunt Pomponia, being converted prior to St. Paul's visit to Rome, the rest of the British royal family, Brân, Caractacus, Cyllinus and Cynon, were converted and baptized by St. Paul himself during his detention in that city preceding his first trial. That the palace of Pudens and Claudia was the home of St. Paul and the other apostles; that their four children, Timotheus, Novatus, Pudentiana and Praxedes, were instructed in the faith by St. Paul; and that Linus, the brother of Claudia and second son of Caractacus, was appointed by the same apostle first bishop of the Church of Rome, such Church meeting at that time, and till the reign of Constantine, in the aforesaid palace, called indifferently " Domus Pudentis, Palatium, Britannicum, Domus Apostolorum, Titulus, Pastor, St. Pudentiana."

13. That after the return of Caractacus to Siluria, St. Paul himself, following the footsteps of his bishop and forerunner, Aristobulus, visited Britain, and confirmed the British Churches in the faith.

14. That the last days of St. Paul, preceding his martyrdom at Rome, were attended by Pudens, Claudia, Linus, Eubulus, whose salutations he sends in his dying charge to Timothy, and that his remains were interred by them in their family sepulchre.

15. That the foundations of the British Church were Apostolical, being coeval, within a few years, with those of the Pentecostal Church at Jerusalem, —preceding those of the primitive Church of Rome,

so far as they were laid by either an apostle or apostolic bishop, by seven years,—preceding the arrival of St. Peter at Rome, as fixed by the great majority of Roman Catholic historians (thirteenth year of Nero), by thirty years,—preceding the first arrival of the papal Church of Rome in Britain, under Augustine, by 456 years.

16. That the British Church has from its origin been a royal one; the royal family of ancient Britain,—of whom our present sovereign is, through the Tudors, the lineal blood representative—being 1. the first British converts to Christianity; 2. the founders of the first Christian institutions in Britain; 3. the chief instruments, in the second century, in the establishment of Christianity as the state religion; and in the fourth century, in the persons of Helen and Constantine the Great, the chief instrument in the aboliton of Paganism, and the substitution, in its place, of Christianity over the whole Roman Empire.

17. That the spiritual or ecclesiastical head of the British Church was always a Briton, resident in Britain, amenable to British laws, and British laws only, and having no superior in the Church but Christ.

18. That whatever may be the religious advantages or disadvantages of the union of the ecclesiastical and civil governments in the person of the Sovereign, such union has been, from the first colonization of our Island, first in Druidic and then in Christian times, the native British, as opposed to the foreign papal—and, in later times, dissenting—principle of their separation.

finis

HORACE KNOWLES

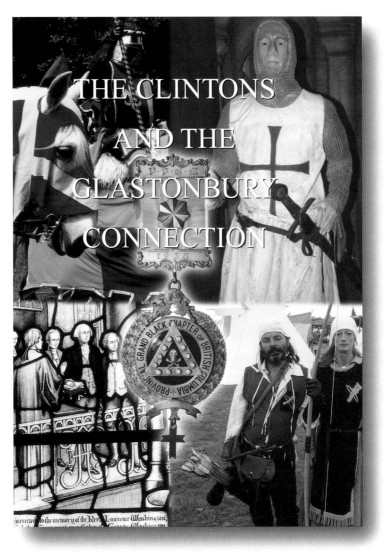

Ronald Rayner
www.theclintonconnection.com   ISBN: 978-0-955-7906-0-7

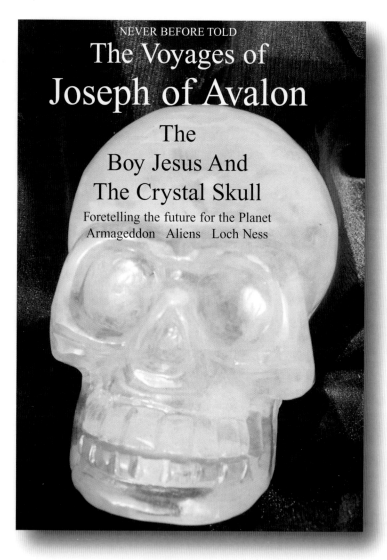

NEVER BEFORE TOLD
The Voyages of
Joseph of Avalon
The
Boy Jesus And
The Crystal Skull
Foretelling the future for the Planet
Armageddon   Aliens   Loch Ness

Ronald Rayner
www.josephofavalon.com   ISBN: 978-0-955-7906-1-4